PAUL J. SACHS

Paul J. Sachs.

MEMORIAL EXHIBITION

WORKS OF ART FROM

THE COLLECTION OF

PAUL J. SACHS

[1878-1965]

GIVEN AND BEQUEATHED TO THE

FOGG ART MUSEUM

HARVARD UNIVERSITY

CAMBRIDGE, MASSACHUSETTS

Distributed by
NEW YORK GRAPHIC SOCIETY
GREENWICH, CONNECTICUT

Acknowledgments

The catalogue has been compiled by Agnes Mongan with the assistance of Mary Lee Bennett. We are grateful for the help of Frances Cohen, Marjorie Benedict Cohn, Usher P. Coolidge, Catherine Scott Coté, Carol Collins Gillham, Elizabeth Hoover, Bernice Park Jones, Max Loehr, Melissa McQuillan, Ruth Magurn, Marjorie Markel, Eliza Mason, David G. Mitten, Elizabeth Mongan, Sarah Richardson, Seymour Slive, Elisabeth Strassmann, Stuart C. Welch, H. Wade White, Peter A. Wick, Eunice Williams, Dorothy Usher Wilson and many others.

Cambridge, Fogg Art Museum, November 15, 1965–January 15, 1966

New York, Museum of Modern Art, December 19, 1966–February 26, 1967

Foreword

Although Paul Sachs will be remembered for many things, during his life he was best known for his achievements as a director of the Fogg Museum. What made these achievements possible were his talents as a counselor, a teacher, a friend and an administrator, but especially his capacity to harmonize the diversity of his gifts. Collecting provided the focus. It requires discrimination, and this quality was the foundation of that good advice he gave so widely and so well. For some, teaching is based on the ordering of facts, for others, on the propounding of hypotheses. His was inspired by the true collector's passion for objects. But however intense, his love of works of art never ended with himself. It was always a means, first to achieve, then to convey understanding. Hence, rising as it did above mere personal predilection, this love of works of art could on the one hand provide a bond with his innumerable friends, and on the other illumine the central educational purpose of a University Art Museum.

Gradually and gracefully, over twenty years, Paul Sachs withdrew from the concerns to which he had devoted his life. Each relinquishment posed a challenge to those whose good fortune it was to take over the activities his wisdom had directed, his enthusiasm had made thrive, and his generosity had sustained. But from collecting and his collections he never retired. So, until the checklist which accompanies this catalogue was prepared, neither his family nor his closest professional associates were aware of the range of his artistic interests or the extent of his donations. Until the finest works of art he had collected were here for the first time put on display no one could grasp how sure and how profound was his perception of quality.

Yet to those who knew Paul Sachs even this exhibition and its catalogue will seem but inert records. To us he left a more vital legacy. His capacity to recognize and understand beauty, his determination to preserve and to make available that beauty, his gift to communicate and his delight in communicating that understanding, these qualities have created for us a fresh image of goodness and have established for all a new definition of greatness.

JOHN COOLIDGE

Introduction

When Paul J. Sachs arrived in Cambridge, in the early autumn of 1915, to take up his post as assistant director of the Fogg Museum, he had had no museum experience whatsoever. His appointment had been proposed and supported by that imaginative planner, Edward W. Forbes, who, in 1909, had succeeded Charles H. Moore as the museum's director. Mr. Forbes had called upon his somewhat younger colleague-to-be (there was a five-year difference of age between them) in New York and convinced the younger man that there was a place in Cambridge for which he was eminently qualified. Although not without qualms concerning those qualifications, Paul Sachs was tremendously excited by the prospect and eager to make the change.

Samuel Sachs reconciled himself to the inevitable and released the eldest of his three sons from his position as a partner in the family banking firm of Goldman Sachs. The elder Mr. Sachs had until then hoped that Paul would follow in his own footsteps.

It was with high hopes and tremendous anticipation of a full and different life that the thirty-seven-year-old ex-banker moved his devoted wife and three small daughters to Cambridge. These hopes were to be more than fulfilled.

If, in one sense, Paul Sachs had no precise professional training for the place he was to assume (one might ask who had at that point in our history), in another sense he had been preparing for it all his life. As a boy he had covered the walls of his room with reproductions. As a young man he had begun his print collection. During the years following his graduation from Harvard (Class of 1900), both in New York and on his business trips abroad, he had visited all the great public and private collections to which he could gain access. Saturdays, accompanied by Mrs. Sachs, he had haunted the dealers and any special art exhibitions which were open. Early in life he had become an avid art book and photograph collector.

When he received official confirmation from Harvard of his appointment, which was to begin in September, 1915, he spent the first half of that year abroad, chiefly in Italy, seeing and learning as much as he could before the fall term began.

His first year at Harvard was devoted solely to the museum, not to teaching. The following academic year, 1916-17, he gave his first fine arts lectures—at Wellesley where he had been appointed "Lecturer in Art." A Harvard appointment in the Department of Fine Arts quickly followed. In 1917 he was made an assistant professor. The double association, as a museum administrator and as a member of the Department of Fine Arts—he became a full professor in 1927 and chairman of the department in 1933 and associate director of the museum from 1923 until his retirement—continued until 1945. That year both men retired from the museum, but Mr. Sachs continued three years longer as Professor.

The exciting quality of Paul Sachs's teaching, his contagious enthusiasm, his instantaneous reaction to an object of quality, no matter of what school or place, and his capacity to make his students see and feel that quality, a long generation of former students knows without being told. We have spoken about it elsewhere, as we have spoken about his unique Museum Course and the influence that his discerning judgment of men and situations has had upon the museum profession throughout the United States ("Paul J. Sachs," *Art Journal,* Vol. xxv, No. 1, Fall 1965).

Some of his former students will remember his love of one school or one type of object, others will remember his tremendous enthusiasm for something else. Almost no one, except possibly Edward Forbes, will have suspected the real breadth of his taste. Few can have surmised the extent of his generosity, although day after day and year after year individual students were aware of it, as he welcomed them to his house, lent them his books, gave them letters of introduction, and in many cases anonymously helped to finance their studies or their travels.

The present exhibition is to honor his memory and demonstrate his generosity. The choice will show as well, it is hoped, something of the scope and quality of his collecting, the degree of his accomplishment, and the influence of his taste. Until preparations for it were begun, no complete list of his gifts had ever been prepared. In fact no count of his prints, his gifts in just one, but the most numerous, category had ever been taken. There was a good reason for this. While he was attached to the Fogg Museum, at his express command, no label bore his name, whether as lender or donor. Many an object, familiar, loved and famous, that has borne for decades a label such as that, for example, on the painting by the Osservanza Master, *Christ in Limbo,* "Gift of a Friend of the Fogg" can now be known as a gift of Paul J. Sachs (Pl. 87).

His gifts to the museum began before his arrival in Cambridge. His first was prophetic in two ways, for it showed not only the quality of his taste but the category in which he was to achieve pre-eminent status, the graphic arts. That gift was the etching by Rembrandt *The Great Jewish Bride* (Pl. 94). He presented it to the Print Room in 1911, a year before he was appointed to the museum's Visiting Committee, and four years before he moved to Cambridge. Over the years his gifts of prints continued to flow in. Early he had reasoned that, with a good eye and a modest fortune—and he had deliberately chosen against a large fortune —a distinguished collection of prints could be made, prints by some of the greatest masters in the history of art. So he began slowly to acquire them, increasing his knowledge with each purchase. When he moved to Cambridge he was already a confirmed print man. He often also made gifts of fine prints to the Museum of Fine Arts in Boston.

For a number of years he gave what was known as the Print Course. Many of the prints he purchased after his move to Cambridge were acquired as examples for his students. One has only to scan the list at the end of the catalogue to see how wide he cast his net to haul in, from a diversity of European schools, the rare, the unusual and the significant things. For example, there are sixteen woodcuts by Cranach, six rare woodcuts of the Swiss artist Urs Graf, twenty prints by the great master Hans Holbein the Younger, the woodcuts of the charming German called the Master of the Celtis Illustrations, a large number of eighteenth-century French etchings, and, to bring the examples closer to home, twelve etchings by Edward Hopper. This is the barest sampling of his gifts of prints which in its total reaches the enormous figure of 2,012 items. The catholicity of taste shown in that total is even more astounding. He is proved a very enlightened collector of all periods of graphic art. His profound but modest and never-pedantic knowledge he enthusiastically shared, with never-ending courtesy, with other collectors, both neophytes and old hands. He made print collecting a rewarding field not only for himself but for all serious students or collectors who partook of his interest in a very specialized field.

From 1935 until 1955, he was often joined by another notable print collector, the Bostonian Russell Allen. W. G. Russell Allen (1882-1955) was shy, learned and enlightened, with a passionate love and understanding of the various print media. The negotiations, never completed, for the acquisition of the Albertina Collection brought the two men close together in the autumn and winter of 1935. From then on, until Russell Allen's death twenty years later, the short Paul Sachs (five feet) and the tall Russell Allen (6 feet 4 inches) made a picturesque pair as, at home and abroad, they happily ventured forth together, in search of new graphic work of quality and significance.

On that trip to Italy undertaken in 1915, just before he assumed his duties as assistant director of the Fogg Museum, he had made a few outstanding acquisitions not in the print field. For example, he had bought a Greek Head (fourth century B.C.) in Rome, and the *Christ in Limbo,* mentioned above, in London. On his return to New York he had persuaded his father to purchase the unfinished Tintoretto *Allegory of Fidelity* (Pl. 90), as he later persuaded him to acquire the two Poussins, the *Holy Family* (Pl. 91) and the *Birth of Bacchus* (Pl. 92), three paintings which his mother later presented to the Fogg Museum in her husband's memory. They are included in the present exhibition because Paul Sachs chose them, anticipating that one day they would undoubtedly become a permanent part of the Fogg's collection. After 1915 paintings or sculpture of comparable quality and importance were, with a few notable exceptions, to be beyond his means.

In the early twenties his concern began to embrace the field of drawings as well as prints. His visits to Léon Bonnat in the latter's Paris studio and his presence at the Degas Sales where he marveled at the French officers in their light blue uniforms, briefly away from the front, bidding enthusiastically for the drawings as they came up, made deep impressions on him. He, too, in wartime Paris had wished to make an acquisition, this time neither a print nor a drawing. He saw a beautiful sculptured head in a dealer's window. He knew neither the dealer (although they later became warm friends) nor the school to which the head belonged, but he yearned to own it. Before he could assemble the funds to buy it, he was ordered to report at Rheims. When he returned to Paris the head was gone, sold he suspected "to the trade." The memory of it haunted him. He not only kept an eye out for it, but told Denman W. Ross about it and asked the latter also to be on the lookout. His supposition was correct. The Khmer Head turned up in the New York market. This time, although the price was higher, he did not hesitate. He bought it (Pl. 80).

A few other paintings and sculptures he also bought in London at the close of the war, but gradually almost all his emphasis and enthusiasm was directed towards drawings by the old and modern masters. There can be no doubt that in this field he was the pace setter in the United States. The Vanderbilt drawings at the Metropolitan Museum and the Fairfax Murray drawings at the Morgan Library had both been acquired "en bloc." Every drawing that entered the Sachs Collection was individually and lovingly chosen, and selected with such passion and enthusiasm that a whole generation of private collectors and museum curators caught the infection and began to follow his example. Many new museum curators had been members of the Museum Class or had taken the Print Course. When they became active in museums of their own, often their first exhibition was of prints or drawings. They turned to Paul Sachs for loans, loans which were almost never refused.

Many of his friends were now trustees of art museums, newly founded or seeking new aims and new staff and they came to him for advice. He never failed to have ideas for development or suggestions for staff. He was one of the seven founders of the Museum of Modern Art. Alfred H. Barr, Jr., was his suggestion as its first director. William Lieberman, the Curator of Graphic Arts, had been his student. It was characteristic of PJS, as he was affectionately called, that a few days after that museum opened its doors in 1929, he should give it its first drawing, the *Portrait of Anna Peter* by George Grosz (Pl. 70), kindly lent to this exhibition (the only loan) by the Museum of Modern Art. The Trustees later presented him with a Degas drawing for the Fogg, a copy after a sixteenth-century French drawing, which had come to them in the Lillie Bliss Bequest. Happily a year before he died, the new print and drawing galleries at the Museum of Modern Art, named in his honor, were completed.

If, in the late thirties and early forties, his acquisitions diminished in number, it was because works of great quality were becoming harder and harder to find, and the increasing number of grandchildren were a greater and more joyous distraction.

These were the years that saw the preparation and publication of the Fogg catalogue of drawings, the *Pocket Book of Great Drawings* and, as late as 1954, *Modern Prints and Drawings*. They were also the years in which he gradually withdrew from the tremendously active life he had followed for many years, when as a valued board member he had been influential in forming the plans and policies of many an organization.

The hundred objects reproduced in this catalogue, all but one his gift or bequest to the Fogg Museum, show him only as an art collector. He was a great collector and a connoisseur in two fields. One was briefly mentioned above: books relating to the Fine Arts. The other was friendship.

It has proved not feasible to count the books. About 4,000 came in one year at the peak of his giving, when he and Mrs. Sachs gave up that house which had been literally a small center of civilization: Shady Hill; but thousands had come before and thousands more came after that cresting wave. The last came as bequests with the closing of his apartment a few months ago.

When he returned to Cambridge after the First World War there were fewer than 500 photographs and less than 1,000 slides in the old Fogg. When the "new Fogg" opened in June 1927, a building his enthusiasm and vision and that of Mr. Forbes had helped to make a reality, there were nearly 20,000 slides and 50,000 photographs. The library grew in comparable numbers, helped not only by his gifts but the gifts of many others who had caught his fever, and the support of the University which had come to recognize the value of such an adjunct to a teaching institution. The fact that this year the slides have passed the 100,000 mark, the photographs are nearly to the 300,000 and the books in the now-combined Fogg and Harvard Fine Arts Library are up to the 100,000 figure indicates that what he saw well started has continued to grow.

Of his friendships it is impossible to write briefly. A glance at his choice of drawings can be revealing. In the selection of seventy-five drawings from five centuries there are only six pure landscapes. It was not that he disliked landscape. It was rather that he loved and was fascinated by people, not people *en masse* but individuals of all ranks, all nations, all callings. He could be held as spellbound by the life of the simple Gaelic-speaking gardener as he was by that of the most *arriviste* tycoon. Such was his warmth and interest that doors were eagerly opened to receive him whenever he traveled, whether in this country or abroad. But he was happiest receiving, with Mrs. Sachs, a congenial gathering of old and tested companions in his own hospitable house, where the talk was intimate if widely ranging and the fare was distinguished.

It was the fall of 1928. The writer, fresh from a year of graduate study abroad, had been interviewed and accepted for her first and, as it turned out, her only post. As she rose to leave, Professor Sachs had a final word. "I shall *never*," he said (and he was quite as good as his word), "ask you what hours you are keeping or how you are spending your time. I shall assume that as long as you work for us, wherever you are and whatever you are doing, you are working for the good of the Fogg Museum." It was not until long afterwards that it suddenly dawned that what he had in fact given was not an admonition but an accurate description of his own *modus vivendi*.

AGNES MONGAN

Compilers' Note

In preparing this exhibition, every drawing was removed from its frame and re-examined. Every drawing has also been rephotographed. An attempt has been made to give thoroughly accurate descriptions of the media used. In those cases in which the description here given does not tally with that of the Mongan-Sachs Catalogue of 1940, this later one should be favored. Each drawing has been re-measured. In some cases, in the light of new information, titles have been changed. The new measurements and titles now officially supplant previous ones.

We have not repeated the bibliographical and exhibition references previously published but limited our entries to what has appeared since 1940, or in the case of those drawings which went to Europe in 1948, to what has appeared since then. There is a single exception, Friedrich Winkler's *Dürer* which was published in Berlin in 1939, but was not yet in this country when the first edition of the catalogue went to press.

References to loan exhibitions have been included only if there was a published catalogue. We have not counted check lists or mimeographed catalogues. Many of the drawings have been shown in places as widely scattered as Waterville, Maine, Mobile, Alabama, and Phoenix, Arizona, but the exhibitions of which they were part had no catalogues; therefore, they are not mentioned. The Lugt number is given only when the collector's mark actually appears on the drawing.

The number given each drawing will indicate whether it came to the Fogg Museum as a gift or as part of the bequest. All drawings bearing numbers beginning with 1965 are part of the bequest which Mr. Sachs wished to have known henceforth as the Meta and Paul J. Sachs Bequest.

The following bibliographical abbreviations have been used:

Ames   Winslow Ames, *Drawings of the Masters: Italian Drawings from the 15th to the 19th Century,* New York, 1963.

Briquet   C. M. Briquet, *Les Filigranes, dictionnaire historique des marques du papier, dès leur apparition vers 1282 jusqu'en 1600,* 2nd ed., 4 vols., Leipzig, 1923.

Detroit, 1951   Detroit, Detroit Institute of Arts, 1951, *French Drawings of Five Centuries from the Collection of the Fogg Art Museum.*

Lugt   Frits Lugt, *Les Marques de collections de dessins et d'estampes,* Amsterdam, 1921, Supplement, 1956.

Mongan-Sachs   Agnes Mongan and Paul J. Sachs, *Drawings in the Fogg Museum of Art,* Cambridge, 1940, 2 vols.

Moskowitz (I, II or III)	Ira Moskowitz (ed.), *Great Drawings of All Time,* New York, 1962. Vol. I, Italian, Winslow Ames. Vol. II, German, Flemish, Dutch; O. Benesch, J. G. van Gelder, E. Haverkamp-Begemann, F. Lugt. Vol. III, French, A. Mongan.
Paris, 1955	Paris, Musée de l'Orangerie, 1955, *De David à Toulouse Lautrec, chefs-d'oeuvre des collections americaines.*
Rotterdam, Paris, New York	Rotterdam, Boymans Museum, Paris, Musée de l'Orangerie, New York, Museum of Modern Art, 1958-1959, French Drawings from American Collections, Clouet to Matisse. Editions of the catalogue were published in Rotterdam, Paris and New York. Our references are to the French edition since the Dutch and English ones are out of print.
Rosenberg	Jakob Rosenberg, *Great Draughtsmen from Pisanello to Picasso,* Cambridge, 1959.
Sachs, 1951	Paul J. Sachs, *The Pocket Book of Great Drawings,* New York, 1951.
Sachs, 1954	Paul J. Sachs, *Modern Prints and Drawings,* New York, 1954.
San Francisco, 1940	San Francisco, Palace of Fine Arts, Golden Gate International Exposition, 1940, Master Drawings, An Exhibition of Drawings from American Museums and Private Collections.
San Francisco, 1947	San Francisco, California, Palace of the Legion of Honor, 1947, 19th-Century French Drawings.
Shoolman-Slatkin	Regina Shoolman and Charles E. Slatkin, *Six Centuries of French Master Drawings in America,* New York, 1950.
Tietze	Hans Tietze, *European Master Drawings in the United States,* New York, 1947.
Watrous	James Watrous, *The Craft of Old-Master Drawings,* Madison, Wisconsin, 1957.

Paul Joseph Sachs

1878   November 24. Born in New York City, the son of Samuel and Louisa (Goldman) Sachs. Prepared at Sachs' School, New York

1900   Degree: A.B. Harvard

1904   January 14. Married Meta Pollak, New York City

1904-14   Partner, Banking Firm of Goldman, Sachs Co., New York

1912-13   Committee to Visit the Fogg Museum; in 1913 became Chairman

1915   Moved to Cambridge

1915-23   Assistant Director, Fogg Art Museum

1916-17   Lecturer in Art, Wellesley College

1917-22   Assistant Professor of Fine Arts, Harvard

1918   American Red Cross, France, with rank of Captain and then Major

1922   Associate Professor of Fine Arts, Harvard

1923   Associate Director of the Fogg Museum

1923-24   Executive Vice-Chairman, with Bishop William Lawrence and Dean Wallace B. Donham of the $10,000,000 campaign "to develop the University service"

1927   Professor of Fine Arts

1929   Lowell Lecturer

1932-33   Exchange Professor in France, Berlin and Bonn

1933-44   Chairman, Department of Fine Arts, Harvard

1940-63   Administrative Board, Dumbarton Oaks, Washington and Historic Monuments in Europe

1948   July 1. Became Professor Emeritus and Honorary Curator of Drawings of the Fogg Art Museum

1949   Left Shady Hill

1965   February 17. Died in Cambridge

Author: Early Italian Engravings, 1915
Drawings in the Fogg Art Museum 1940 (in collaboration)
Great Drawings 1951
Modern Prints and Drawings 1954

Served terms as Trustee of:
>   Smith College
>   Cincinnati Museum
>   Ella Plotz Foundation for Advancement of Medical Science
>   Museum of Fine Arts, Boston
>   Museum of Modern Art, New York
>   Wellesley College
>   Radcliffe College
>   Beth Israel Hospital, New York
>   New York Foundation
>   National Urban League

Visiting Committees:
>   Department of Fine Arts, Harvard
>   Department of Art and Archaeology, Princeton

Member: Associate of Yale
>   Harvard-Princeton Fine Arts Club (President)
>   American Association of Museums (President)
>   American Federation of Art
>   Association of Art Museum Directors
>   College Art Association (Vice-President)
>   Archaeological Institute of America
>   Medieval Academy of America
>   Syndics of Harvard University Press (Chairman)
>   Art Bulletin, Editorial Board 1919-40

Honorary Societies:
>   American Academy of Arts and Sciences
>   Legion of Honor (Officer)
>   Phi Beta Kappa

Honorary Degrees:
>   University of Pittsburgh
>   Colby College
>   Yale
>   Princeton

THE CATALOGUE

ANONYMOUS GERMAN Late 14th Century

1 Two Designs for Illuminated Initials

Pen and ink, and brush, with touches of vermilion tempera, on parchment. Knight: 5⅜ x 2⅜ in. (135 x 60 mm.) Lady: 5 x 1¾ in. (128 x 44 mm.)   1954.127

No further letters of the alphabet series to which these two drawings belong have turned up since we discussed them in the 1940 catalogue. A letter A that clearly belongs with them is in the Ashmolean Museum, Oxford. Two drawings, cut at the sides in a fashion similar to these, are in the Lewis Randall Collection, Montreal. Experts still do not agree on the place of origin of the series. Dr. K. G. Boon (visit, 1959) suggested a date after 1360. Dr. Hanns Swarzenski believes that they come from Southeast Germany, not Bohemia (conversation, August 26, 1965).

PROVENANCE: Eugène Rodrigues Sale, Frederik Muller's, Amsterdam, July 12-13, 1921, no. 231, pl. LXXVIII; Steinmeyer to Paul J. Sachs.

BIBLIOGRAPHY: Mongan-Sachs, no. 366, figs. 184 and 185.

BENOZZO GOZZOLI (Follower?) Florence 1420–
Pistoia 1497

2 Study for a Flying Figure with Outstretched Arms, and, Below, Studies of Each Hand

Pen and bistre wash heightened with white on brown prepared paper.
$8\frac{7}{16}$ x $6\frac{13}{16}$ in. (214 x 173 mm.)   1958.285

The drawing has long borne an attribution to Gozzoli, but Berenson was not convinced that it was by that master himself. He found the contours a little dry and hard for that engaging and imaginative pictorial painter. He suggested Bartolommeo Caporali of Perugia as its possible author. Others continued to accept the traditional attribution. Recently (in 1958 and again in 1965), however, Philip Pouncey has rejected the Benozzo attribution, also ruling out the possibility that it is by either Caporali or Bonfigli, two Central Italian painters strongly influenced by the Florentine master's work in Umbria. He assigns it, however, to that region. The Fogg Museum received in the Loeser Bequest a sixteenth-century copy of this drawing (Mongan-Sachs Catalogue, no. 17).

PROVENANCE: A. Köster, Boerner Sale Catalogue, Leipzig, November 13, 1924, no. 35, as anonymous Italian; A. G. B. Russell, London; Saville Gallery, Ltd., London, 1929, Sale Catalogue, no. 40; Agnew to Paul J. Sachs, May 25, 1929.

BIBLIOGRAPHY: Mongan-Sachs, no. 16, fig. 18.
                Moskowitz, I, no. 40.
                Ames, p. 40, pl. 8.

EXHIBITIONS: San Francisco, 1940, no. 46, reprod. p. 43.
                Northampton, Smith College, 1941, Italian Drawings, 1330-1780, no. 29.
                Santa Barbara, Museum of Art, 1964, European Drawings, 1450-1900, no. 1.

ANTONIO DEL POLLAIUOLO

Florence 1432/33–Rome 1498

3 Fighting Nudes

Pen and bistre and bistre wash. 10⅝ x 7⅟₁₆ in. (270 x 180 mm.)   1940.9

There seems little to add to the lengthy discussion of the puzzling meaning of this drawing and its significance for Florentine art. This has been
explored in the Mongan-Sachs catalogue. An examination under high
magnification of a copy of the engraving related to the drawing revealed
that a deft restorer had made hitherto unsuspected additions in pen to
the engraving. This suggested that a similar examination of the drawing should be made, and it was done. When the drawing was then com-
pared to the facsimile of it, published while the drawing was still at
Wilton House, it became clear that between the time that reproduction
had been made and the time Paul Sachs acquired the drawing, it too had
passed through the hands of a very clever and accomplished restorer. But
the drawing, one of great rarity and historic importance, rightly remained one of the purchases of which Paul Sachs was most proud.

PROVENANCE: Jonathan Richardson, Sr. (1665-1745); the Earl of Pembroke
Sale, Sotheby's, July 9, 1917, no. 343; Knoedler to Paul J. Sachs.

BIBLIOGRAPHY: Mongan-Sachs, no. 37, fig. 33.
Helen Comstock, Review of above, *Connoisseur,* September,
1947, p. 39, reprod.
Tietze, no. 12, reprod.
Moskowitz, I, pl. 14.
Ames, p. 44, pl. 12.

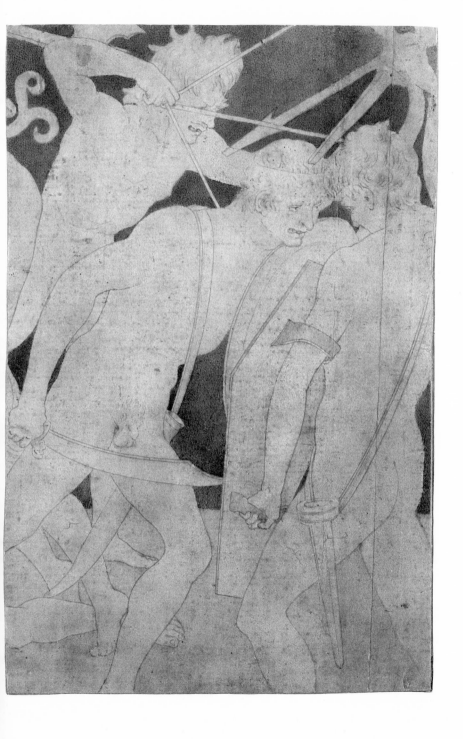

ANDREA MANTEGNA Padua 1431–Mantua 1506

4 Eight Apostles Watching the Ascension of Christ

Quill pen and bistre outlines with brush wash (faded) heightened with white on grey-green prepared paper. $11\frac{3}{8}$ x $8\frac{1}{2}$ in. (290 x 218 mm.) Inscription at lower right in a nineteenth-century hand: Mantegna

1926.42.1

The drawing has long been known as *Seven Apostles*. In a paper submitted to the Department of Fine Arts in 1962, Robert Munman pointed out that actually there are eight apostles represented, as there are in the painting of 1464 in the Uffizi for which the drawing served as a *modello*. He reported extensively on the condition of the drawing, also noting that the figure of the Madonna can be discerned in close examination. The white at the bottom is a restoration. The recent cleaning of the Hampton Court *Triumph* has revealed that Mantegna handled his highlights there very much in the manner of those in this drawing.

PROVENANCE: Moscardo; Luigi Grassi (Lugt Suppl. 1171[b]); gift of Mrs. Jesse I. Straus to Paul J. Sachs for the Fogg Museum, Florence, 1926.

BIBLIOGRAPHY: Mongan-Sachs, no. 24, fig. 25.
Jean Cassou, "Demarche of the Creative Thought," *Gazette des Beaux-Arts,* XXXIII, 1948, p. 242.
Helen Gardner, *Art Through the Ages,* New York, 1959, p. 13.
Moskowitz, 1, pl. 69.

EXHIBITIONS: Philadelphia, Art Museum, 1950-51, Masterpieces of Drawing, no. 13.

FILIPPINO LIPPI   Prato ca. 1457–Florence 1504

5   A Female Figure Leaning Forward and a Figure of a Kneeling Man

Brush (or pen) with bistre, heightened with white on grey prepared paper. 8¾ x 7½ in. (222 x 190 mm.)   1965.394

The drawing, formerly erroneously described as in silverpoint, seems to have been done with a fine brush or soft pen. Berenson believed it contemporary with the Esther panels, that is between 1472 and 1480. Filippino often drew on paper prepared with different grounds, rose, violet, grey and blue; and generally on the colored grounds he used a silverpoint. This drawing would seem to be an exception.

PROVENANCE: B. Grahame (1878); E. J. Poynter Sale, Sotheby's, April 24-25, 1918, no. 74 (Lugt 874); Colnaghi to Paul J. Sachs.

BIBLIOGRAPHY: Mongan-Sachs, no. 21, fig. 20.

EXHIBITIONS: San Francisco, 1940, no. 66, reprod. p. 32.

PERUGINO, Pietro Vannucci called

Castello della Pieve 1446–Fontignano 1523

6 Four Standing Apostles

Black chalk and brown ink heightened with white lead on white paper which has faded to tan. 11⅜ x 8⅞ in. (290 x 225 mm.)
In ink at lower right edge, a sixteenth-century (?) inscription: Pietro Perugino 38   1926.42.2

The drawing is a study for a large altarpiece of the Ascension, the central panel of which is now in the museum at Lyons. The altarpiece was commissioned on March 8, 1495, by the Benedictines of San Pietro, Perugia. The central part was finished in 1496. The painting was a great success and Perugino and his assistants repeated it at least four times. Probably the drawing remained in the workshop. Assistants and followers copied the whole group or separate figures. None of the copies or variants is as clearly, firmly and delicately drawn as the Sachs drawing.

PROVENANCE: Sale, Hôtel Drouot, Paris, May 16, 1923, no. 81; Jacques Auguste Boussac Sale (Mons. J. B.), Sotheby's, London, July 9, 1924, no. 178, reprod.; given by Mrs. Jesse I. Straus to Paul J. Sachs for the Fogg Museum, 1926.

BIBLIOGRAPHY: Mongan-Sachs, no. 28, fig. 26.
Sachs, 1951, p. 34, pl. 21.
Luigi Grassi, *I disegni italiani del Trecento e Quattrocento,* Sodalizio del Libro, Venice, 1961, p. 218, pl. 108.
Henry S. Francis, "Three Early Italian Drawings," *Bulletin of the Cleveland Museum of Art,* XLIX, September, 1962, p. 171.

EXHIBITIONS: Newark, Newark Museum, 1960, Old Master Drawings, 1960, no. 5, reprod.

Pietro Perugino   38

BERNARDINO PINTURICCHIO

Perugia 1454–Siena 1513

7 Group of Six Seated and Seven Standing Figures

Brush and bistre on paper faded to an ivory tone, restored in upper and lower right corners; the profile of the seated figure, second from the right, strengthened by a later hand. 9⅞ x 7 in. (250 x 170 mm.)

1965.408

The drawing, one of the very few which can with any confidence be attributed to Pinturicchio, is fascinating not only for its vitality and delicacy, but also because of its exotically dressed personalities and its suggestion of solemn ceremonial. Naturally it recalls Pinturicchio's bright and elaborate decorations for the Piccolomini Chapel, Siena, and the Borgia apartments at the Vatican. Since the lengthy discussion in the Mongan-Sachs catalogue, new data has not come to light.

PROVENANCE: Sir J. C. Robinson; Colnaghi to Paul J. Sachs, 1927.

BIBLIOGRAPHY: Mongan-Sachs, no. 34, fig. 30.
Augusta Ghidiglia Quintavalle, "Alessandro Araldi," *Rivista dell'instituto nazionale di archeologia e storia dell'arte,* n.s. VII, 1958, p. 310.
Luigi Grassi, *I disegni italiani del Trecento e Quattrocento,* Sodalizio del Libro, Venezia, 1961, p. 221, pl. 112.
Ames, p. 100, pl. 68.

EXHIBITIONS: Poughkeepsie, Vassar College, 1956, Humanism North and South, no. 11.

FRA BARTOLOMMEO Florence 1472–Pian di Mugnone 1517

8 Madonna and Child with a Kneeling Angel

Pen and brown ink on white paper faded to tan. $5\frac{5}{16}$ x $7\frac{7}{8}$ in. (151 x 200 mm.)

Watermark: Six-pointed star in a circle (similar to Briquet 6077 but without the cross)   1965.356

In his early years in the monastery of San Marco, that is between 1500 and 1504, Fra Bartolommeo made countless drawings of the Madonna and Child, inventing an infinite number of charming variations on the theme. During those years a pen was his preferred tool. The scale of the drawings was small, the strokes light and rhythmical, the cross-hatchings deft and delicate, the mood intimate and gracious. Surviving drawings similar to this in mood and handling are preserved at Bayonne, Berlin, Florence, London and Windsor. In them is made visible Fra Bartolommeo's debt to Leonardo and the young Raphael's debt to him. A late copy of the drawing was formerly in the Brandegee Collection, Brookline.

PROVENANCE: William Mayor (Lugt 2799); E. J. Poynter (Lugt 874) Sale, Sotheby's, April 24-25, 1918, no. 12; Colnaghi to Paul J. Sachs, 1925.

BIBLIOGRAPHY: Mongan-Sachs, no. 57, fig. 48.
Charles de Tolnay, *History and Technique of Old Master Drawings,* New York, 1943, p. 117, no. 77, reprod.

EXHIBITIONS: Baltimore, Museum of Art, 1961, Bacchiacca and His Friends, no. 27, reprod.

LUCAS CRANACH the Elder Kronach 1472–
Weimar 1553

9 St. Anthony Abbot

Pen with brown and grey washes on white paper, squared for enlargement. $7\frac{7}{16}$ x $7\frac{1}{2}$ in. (190 x 191 mm.)
Verso: Slight pen sketch for the left half of an altarpiece with indications of an arched predella.   1965.338

The indications of a half-length figure in a hemicycle in the drawing on the verso would seem to indicate that the obverse is a study for a half-length figure in a predella. It dates probably from about 1509-10, and may be connected with the work Cranach was doing at the time for the Castle of Torgau.

PROVENANCE: J. A. G. Weigel; Habich; Brera Gallery, Milan (Deposito Frizzoni); Charles A. Loeser to Paul J. Sachs.

BIBLIOGRAPHY: Mongan-Sachs, no. 376, fig. 191.
Jakob Rosenberg, *Die Zeichnungen Lucas Cranachs, d. Ä.,* Berlin, 1960, no. 10.

EXHIBITIONS: San Francisco, 1940, no. 17, reprod.

HANS LEONARD SCHÄUFELEIN

Nuremberg ca. 1480–Nordlingen 1539/40

10 Adoration of the Magi

Pen with brown and black ink over charcoal on white paper. 9⅜ x 8¾
in. (238 x 223 mm.)
Inscribed by the artist with color notations to the left of the Madonna's
sleeve, on the steps by her skirt, beneath the right arm of the standing
old king and beneath the knee of the kneeling king. Damaged along bottom edge and at the lower corner.   1965.351

When we prepared the entry for the Mongan-Sachs catalogue, we knew
the Innsbruck *Adoration* only through a poor reproduction. An examination of the original (summer 1965) made it seem closer to the drawing
in spirit and in design than we had previously thought. Schäufelein
twice repeated the subject in woodcuts, once for an illustrated gospel of
1512 and once for a *Plenarium* printed in Basel in 1514. For the latter he
made five large woodcut illustrations. Both the 1512 and the 1514 woodcuts show a composition in reverse to the drawing. The Balthasar of 1512
recalls the Balthasar of the drawing, and the elderly kneeling king with
pointed beard of 1514 wears a similar robe, has an identical hat, and
offers the Child a square box. (For reproductions see Maria Consuelo
Oldenbourg's *Die Buchholzschnitte des Hans Schäufelein,* 2 vols., Stras-
bourg, 1964: vol. I, p. 33, no. 221, and p. 64, no. 495; vol. II, plates, pp.
39 and 77.) If the drawing was made in preparation for a woodcut, one
wonders about the color notes on the drawing.

PROVENANCE: Adalbert Freiherr von Lanna (1836-1909) Sale, Gutekunst,
Stuttgart, May 6-11, 1910, no. 495; Keppel to Paul J. Sachs.

BIBLIOGRAPHY: Mongan-Sachs, no. 393, fig. 204.

ALBRECHT DÜRER

Nuremberg 1471 – Nuremberg 1528

11   The Lamentation

Pen and ink on white paper. 11⅜ x 8¼ in. (290 x 210 mm.)
Signed, in sky at upper right, with Dürer's monogram and dated 1521.

1965.339

This well-known and well-loved drawing by one of the greatest of all graphic artists is among the treasures of the museum. It is the single drawing which Paul Sachs discussed at length in his *Pocket Book* (see below). For many years it was also the drawing which Dr. Rosenberg chose to put before his graduate class in connoisseurship when, for the first time, they closely confronted an original work of art and were asked to consider its qualities and importance at every level: technical, iconographical, historical and aesthetic. Thus it is a drawing intimately known to a long generation of students. Winkler, who had not seen the original when he published his work on Dürer's drawings (see below), believed that possibly Dürer made the drawing on his journey to the Netherlands in 1521. He saw no reason to question the date, as Ephrussi had done. He was a little puzzled that such an important drawing had a history that went no further back than the middle of the nineteenth century. He suggested that possibly it was the *Entombment* in the Denon Sale in 1826, no. 607, noting that the entries in Denon's catalogue were summary and occasionally inaccurate. This suggestion we find reasonable.

PROVENANCE: Baron Vivant-Denon(?); Sir Thomas Lawrence; Defer-Dumesnil (Lugt 739); Lebeuf de Mongermont Sale, Georges Petit Gallery, Paris, June 18-19, 1919, no. 232; Féral to Paul J. Sachs.

BIBLIOGRAPHY: Friedrich Winkler, *Die Zeichnungen Albrecht Dürers,* 4 vols., Berlin, 1936-39, IV, pp. 67-68, no. 881, reprod.
Mongan-Sachs, no. 377, fig. 192.
Erwin Panofsky, *A. Dürer,* Princeton, 1945, II, p. 71, no. 609.
Sachs, 1951, pp. 51-53, pl. 33.
Agnes Mongan, "Notes on the History of Drawing," *Journal of the American Association of University Women,* XLIV, January, 1951, pp. 81-86, reprod. p. 82.
Friedrich Winkler, *Albrecht Dürer, Leben und Werk,* Berlin, 1957, p. 328.

ALBRECHT DÜRER

Nuremberg 1471–Nuremberg 1528

12 Susanna of Bavaria (1502-1543)

Soft natural chalk (not metal point) heightened with white on paper prepared with a green ground. $15\frac{7}{8}$ x $11\frac{9}{16}$ in. (403 x 294 mm.)
Watermark: High crown surmounted by a cross, similar to Briquet, nos. 4902 and 4911.
Inscribed in Dürer's hand in ink at upper right: 1525   1949.1

Susanna, the daughter of Duke Albert the Wise and Kunigunda, the sister of Emperor Maximilian I, married first Casimir, Margrave of Kulmbach and a year after his death, that is in 1528, Otto Heinrich of Pfalz-Neuburg. She was described in an eighteenth-century inventory as "Dürer's great protectress." She was still the wife of Casimir when this portrait was drawn. At the beginning of this century the portrait was entitled Margaret of Hohenzollern. Kaiser Wilhelm II was about to acquire it as an ancestral portrait when the First World War broke out. He apparently did not know that Campbell Dodgson had provided a more accurate identification. Paul Sachs loved to recount how he had seen the drawing at Colnaghi's in London on his way to France in 1918, said he would like to have it, and had forgotten about it until, when the war was over, Colnaghi's had written to say they were holding it for him.

PROVENANCE: General Andréossy; Ambroise Firmin-Didot (Lugt 119); J. P. Heseltine; Colnaghi to Paul J. Sachs, November, 1922.

BIBLIOGRAPHY: Friedrich Winkler, *Die Zeichnungen Albrecht Dürers,* Berlin, 1936-39, IV, pp. 84-85, no. 914, reprod.
Mongan-Sachs, no. 378, fig. 193.
Erwin Panofsky, *Albrecht Dürer,* Princeton, 1943, I, p. 240; II, no. 1057, p. 109.
Hans Tietze, *Dürer,* Vienna, 1951, no. 91, reprod.
Friedrich Winkler, *Albrecht Dürer, Leben und Werk,* Berlin, 1957, p. 343.

1525

HANS HOLBEIN the Younger

Augsburg 1497/8–London 1543

13 Head of a Young Man

Natural red and black chalks, quill pen and carbon black ink, with washes of ochre on a laid paper, on a wove paper support. 8⅛ x 6 in. (205 x 152 mm.)

Dated at upper edge in chalk: 1523; inscribed on reverse by Wilhelm Koller: Porträt U. von Hütten in seinem Todesjahr. 1949.2

The drawing has suffered badly from the hand of Time. At some point it was remounted. Since the remounting is on wove paper, it was probably done in the nineteenth century. The inscription on the reverse of the mount by Wilhelm Koller is not to be lightly dismissed. Koller was, according to Lugt, a man of taste and an excellent connoisseur, not the type to create a legend. The fact that von Hütten did die in 1523 lends support to Koller's statement. It is generally agreed that the pen lines are later, but how much later it is impossible to say. Paul Sachs believed them original and, against strong opposition, maintained his opinion. The paper itself has been almost worn away and what remains has been strongly compressed. Much of the grey must also be a later addition. For many years the drawing was called *Portrait of a Leper*. Leprosy was long a generic term for skin diseases. More than one distinguished dermatologist in recent years has diagnosed the young man's ailment as a case of *impetigo contagioso*.

PROVENANCE: Wilhelm Koller the Elder Sale, Vienna, February 5, 1872, 100 fls.; Freiherr von Lanna Sale, Gutekunst, Stuttgart, 1908, no. 234; Max Bonn Sale, Sotheby's, February 15, 1922; Colnaghi to Paul J. Sachs, 1922.

BIBLIOGRAPHY: Mongan-Sachs, no. 386, fig. 196.
Tietze, 1947, p. 74, no. 39, reprod.
Watrous, 1957, pp. 106, 110, reprod. p. 111.
Moskowitz, II, 1962, pl. 437.

EXHIBITIONS: Newark, Newark Museum, 1960, Old Master Drawings, no. 17, reprod.
Basel, Kunstmuseum, 1960, Die Familie Holbein in Basel, p. 256, no. 276, pl. 96.

FRANCESCO PRIMATICCIO

Bologna 1504–Paris 1570

14   An Allegorical Group Representing Astronomy

Red chalk heightened with white on pink paper. 5$\frac{3}{16}$ x 8⅝ in. (132 x 220 mm.)   1959.160

The drawing, probably the finished study for a decorative panel to be executed in grisaille or fresco, cannot be connected with any known surviving work. In style it seems to date after Primaticcio's return from Rome, where he had been sent by François Ier in 1540 after working eight years at Fontainebleau. He returned to France in the winter of 1541 with one hundred and thirty-three cases of works of art for the King. Primaticcio was then put in charge of executing all the royal commands for the decoration of Fontainebleau, as well as the restoration of antiquities, the casting of bronzes, and the manufacture of tapestries and of Limoges enamels. He held this post under four kings. There was so much to do that he generally contented himself with the making of drawings which were turned over to his assistants to be carried out in the various media for which they were intended.

PROVENANCE: Duval le Camus (Lugt 1441); Alphonse Kann to Paul J. Sachs, 1922.

BIBLIOGRAPHY: Mongan-Sachs, no. 149, fig. 285.

EXHIBITIONS: Indianapolis, John Herron Art Institute, 1954, Pontormo to Greco, no. 30, reprod.
Vancouver, Art Gallery, 1964, The Nude in Art, no. 27.

FRANÇOIS CLOUET   Tours ca. 1510–Paris 1572

15   Portrait of Claude Gouffier de Boisy

Natural black and red chalks on white paper. 12⅝ x 9 1/16 in. (320 x 230 mm.)

Watermark: A small crown (not recorded in Briquet)

Inscribed in the upper left in the hand of one of Catherine dei Medici's secretaries "Debosy"; numbered 5, in Ignatius Hugford's writing.

1949.5

Claude Gouffier, Master of the Horse to François Ier was Clouet's protector. This drawing must have been made about 1555, to judge by costume and style. An earlier drawing of him dating ca. 1543 is preserved at Chantilly (Moreau-Nélaton, *Les Clouets et leurs émules,* I, p. 53). A painted portrait at Versailles is about a decade later (Archives Photographiques 3225). There are a number of drawings which bear Hugford's numbering. They all represent court personages close to the household of Catherine dei Medici. Christine of Lorraine inherited the drawings from her godmother, the widowed queen, and carried them to Florence as part of her dowry when she went to Florence to marry the Grand Duke of Tuscany. How they got into Hugford's hands in the eighteenth century can only be surmised. He sold several to English noblemen making the grand tour and so they again traveled north of the Alps.

PROVENANCE: Catherine dei Medici; Christine of Lorraine, Grand Duchess of Tuscany; Ignatius Hugford; Marquis de Biron; Alphonse Kann to Paul J. Sachs, 1918.

BIBLIOGRAPHY: Mongan-Sachs, no. 569, fig. 284.
Shoolman and Slatkin, pl. 8.
Sachs, 1951, p. 78 and pl. 50.
Watrous, p. 104.
Michel W. Alpakov, *Geschichte der Kunst,* II, Dresden, 1964, p. 145.

EXHIBITIONS: Detroit, 1951, no. 2, reprod.
Rotterdam, Paris, New York, 1958-59, no. 6, reprod. no. 5.

PAOLO VERONESE   Verona 1528–Venice 1588

16   The Rest on the Flight into Egypt

Quill pen and bistre heightened with white on blue-green paper. 9¾ x
7¾ in. (248 x 198 mm.)
Watermark: An angel (not in Briquet)   1965.430

According to Carlo Ridolfi, the seventeenth-century historian, Veronese
made many drawings on colored paper which, since they were done
with great artistry and completeness, were as highly valued at the time
as were his paintings. Several such drawings, of which this is one, survive. In its contrast of light and shadow within the three-color limit, the
color of the paper, the wash, and the white highlights, it achieves effects
quite close to those of the chiaroscuro prints so popular in the late sixteenth century. The Nebehay Catalogue noted that a copy of this drawing by Van Dyck is in the Albertina, Vienna. A variant, in the same technique, but with St. Joseph standing at the right and the Madonna facing
three-quarters left, is in the British Museum.

PROVENANCE: Sir Thomas Lawrence; D. G. de Arozarena; Gustave Nebehay
               Sale Catalogue of Drawings, Heft IV, n.d., no. 160, to Paul J.
               Sachs, 1928.

BIBLIOGRAPHY: Mongan-Sachs, no. 204, fig. 111.
               Teitze and E. Teitze-Conrat, *The Drawings of the Venetian
               Painters,* New York, 1944, p. 341, no. 2051.
               Sachs, 1951, pp. 42-43, pl. 28.
               Moskowitz, II, pl. 231.
               Ames, p. 80, pl. 48.

EXHIBITIONS: Hartford, Wadsworth Atheneum, 1948, The Life of Christ, no.
               24.
               Toronto, Art Gallery, 1960, Titian, Tintoretto, Paolo Veronese,
               no. 46.

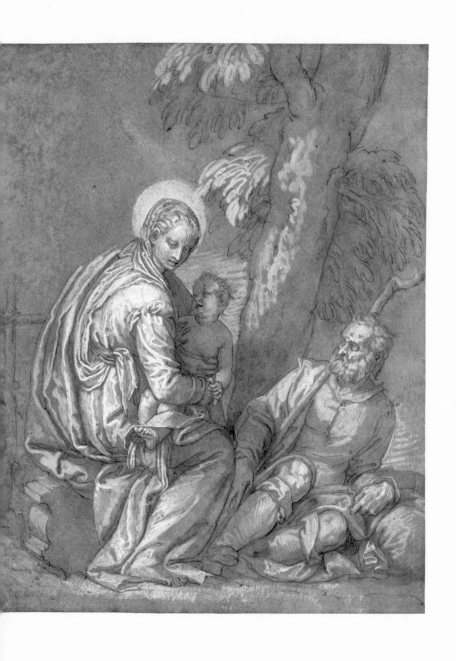

JAKOB DE GHEYN II

Antwerp 1565–The
Hague 1629

17 A Cross-Bowman Assisted by a Milkmaid

Pen with brown ink and grey wash over red chalk indications on off-white paper, traced with a stylus. 15⅜ x 12¾ in. (390 x 323 mm.)

1953.86

The drawing is the preparatory drawing for the print of the same subject, a print accompanied by moralizing verses in Latin and Dutch. The drawing was unknown before 1953. Jakob Rosenberg dates it about 1600, placing it after the military prints of 1596-98, but before de Gheyn's freer work of the sixteen hundreds. In the figures and in its moralizing allegory, it reveals traces of mannerism; in its clean contours, the strict discipline of de Gheyn's master, Goltzius. The landscape, however, is freer, pointing toward the Baroque. The bowman shoots with his left hand because the scene will be reversed in the engraving. A later pen version, in de Gheyn's freer manner and without the landscape, is in the Berlin Print Room. The verses warn that the bowman, with the encouragement of the girl, takes aim against those swelled with pride and pompousness.

PROVENANCE: Blumka Gallery to Paul J. Sachs, 1953.

BIBLIOGRAPHY: Jakob Rosenberg, "A Drawing by Jacques de Gheyn," *Art Quarterly,* Summer 1954, pp. 166-171, reprod.

VENETIAN 17th Century

18 A Triumphant General Crowned by a Flying Figure

Quill pen and bistre wash. 10¾ x 7¾ in. (272 x 197 mm.)   1965.429

This handsome Baroque drawing has remained without an attribution because, although many names have been suggested, none seems to be beyond discussion. Dalton, its earliest known possessor, was librarian at Windsor and agent for George III from the latter's accession in 1760. In that capacity he made many journeys abroad. Possibly because the drawing lacked an attribution even then, it did not become part of the Royal Collection at Windsor. Dr. Pignatti (February, 1961) suggested Francesco Maffei (Vicenza ca. 1620–Padua 1660). He proposed that a comparison be made between our drawing and Maffei's preparatory study in the Albertina (Drawing Catalogue 1947, VI, no. 741) for the painting *St. Charles Borromeo with the Plague Stricken.*

PROVENANCE: R. Dalton (Lugt 354); Boussac; D'Hendecourt; Colnaghi to Paul J. Sachs, May, 1929.

BIBLIOGRAPHY: Mongan-Sachs, no. 301, fig. 144.
Tietze, 1947, no. 46.
Watrous, p. 48.
Moskowitz, II, no. 235.
Ames, p. 119, pl. 87.

EXHIBITIONS: New York, Knoedler and Co., 1959, Great Master Drawings of Seven Centuries, no. 18 (reprod. on cover).

PETER PAUL RUBENS

Siegen(?) 1577–
Château Steen 1640

19   A Study for the Figure of Christ

Black chalk with later outlining in charcoal, heightened with white, re-
inforced at left edge of torso with brush and thin wash, on buff paper.
15¾ x 11¾ in. (400 x 298 mm.)
Watermark: A hunter's horn   1949.3

The drawing is a study for the *Raising of the Cross* painted by Rubens
between the summers of 1609 and 1610 and now in the Antwerp Cathedral. An oil sketch of the composition is in the Gallery of Art, Toronto.
Another figure in the same pose, but not by the same hand came to the
Fogg in the Winthrop Bequest. That drawing has also been attributed
to Rubens, but it is not an attribution generally accepted.

PROVENANCE: Jacob de Wit(?); J. D. Böhm, 1794-1865 (Lugt 1442); Werner
              Weisbach; Goudstikker, Amsterdam, to Paul J. Sachs, 1922.

BIBLIOGRAPHY: Mongan-Sachs, no. 483, fig. 249.
              Tietze, 1947, p. 120, no. 60, reprod.
              J. A. Goris and J. S. Held, *Rubens in America,* New York, 1947,
              no. 61.
              Sachs, 1951, pp. 67-68, pl. 42.
              Jakob Rosenberg, "Rubens Oil Sketches and Drawings," *Art
              Quarterly,* Summer 1956, p. 142.
              L. Burchard and R. A. d'Hulst, *Rubens Drawings,* Brussels,
              1963, 2 vols., I, p. 94, no. 55; II, no. 55, reprod.
              Moskowitz, II, no. 521.

EXHIBITIONS: San Francisco, 1940, no. 91, reprod. p. 56.
              Cambridge, Fogg Art Museum, and New York, Pierpont Mor-
              gan Library, 1956, Drawings and Oil Sketches by Rubens from
              American Collections, pp. 14-15, no. 8, pl. 3.
              Antwerp, Rubenshuis, 1956, Tekeningen van P. P. Rubens, no.
              34, pl. 11.

ANTON VAN DYCK Antwerp 1599–London 1641

20   Don Carlos Coloma (1573-1637)

Natural black chalk, heightened with white chalk on white paper faded
to ivory. $9\frac{1}{2}$ x $7\frac{5}{16}$ in. (242 x 187 mm.)
Inscribed in ink in the lower right corner: A van Dijk; and at the lower
left corner: 1628   1961.150

The portrait is a study for one of the prints in van Dyck's *Iconography,*
a series prepared between 1626, when van Dyck returned from Italy, and
his departure, in 1632, for England. The engraving was made by Paul
Pontius (Mauquoy-Hendrickx, no. 45). In the 1940 catalogue, we noted
the existence of two grisailles. Since then we have learned of a third, in
the collection of the Duke of Buccleugh at Boughton House. The Buccleugh grisaille (Courtauld neg. 1354/306) is more vigorous and lively
than the Bonnat one; indeed, the latter seems probably a copy of it. In
the grisailles, as in the engraving which is in the same direction, Coloma
stands in front of a brocade curtain wearing dress armor, the silk sash
of his rank across his chest, a marshal's baton in his left hand, his mailed
right on a parapet. The hilt of his sword shows at the lower right.
None of this does van Dyck depict, except to give a faint hint of the
angle of the baton. Even the expression of the face is different. Here the
noted Spaniard is less martial and severe in attitude, less the army com-
mander, which he was, than the writer, diplomat and historian which he
became.

PROVENANCE: S. Feitama, Amsterdam; C. A. C. Ponsonby; François Flameng
              (1856-1923) Sale, Georges Petit Gallery, Paris, March 26-27,
              1910, no. 52, reprod.; Agnew to Paul J. Sachs, 1921.

BIBLIOGRAPHY: Mongan-Sachs, no. 466, fig. 238.
              Horst Vey, *Die Zeichnungen Anton van Dycks,* 2 vols., Brussels,
              1962, I, no. 259; II, fig. 312.

EXHIBITIONS: San Francisco, 1940, no. 31, reprod.
              Newark, Newark Museum, 1960, Master Drawings, no. 34.
              Antwerp, Rubenshuis, and Rotterdam, Boymans van Beuningen
              Museum, 1960, Antoon van Dyck *Tekeningen en olieverf-
              schetsen,* no. 83, pp. 120-121 and pl. LIII.

1670.   A van Dijk

ANTON VAN DYCK Antwerp 1599–London 1641

21 Study of Armor

Black chalk and brush with carbon black ink, heightened with white, with green and ochre body color, on beige paper. 14¾ x 9⅞ in. (378 x 352 mm.)   1954.126

For many years this drawing and its companion piece, a view of the same suit of armor from the front, given to the Fogg Museum in 1936 by Ambassador and Mrs. Robert Woods Bliss (Mongan-Sachs, no. 467), bore attributions to van Dyck that were unquestioned. In 1958, Dr. van Regteren Altena suggested that the two drawings might be by Paul de Vos. The Bliss drawing was requested and sent to the great van Dyck drawing exhibition in Antwerp in 1960. At that time, Horst Vey and Roger d'Hulst, the compilers of the catalogue, queried the attributions, suggesting the possibility that the drawing might perhaps be attributed to someone such as Paul de Vos, a specialist, they pointed out, in the painting of armor. They found the rendering rather plastic, uncharacteristic for van Dyck's more fluid line at that period, but did not altogether reject the drawing. They believed the armor itself to be of South German origin, made probably between 1620 and 1640. Other experts who visited the van Dyck exhibition saw no reason to question the traditional attribution.

PROVENANCE: P. H. Lankrink, 1628-92 (Lugt 2090); Lord Lansdowne Sale, Sotheby's, March 20, 1920, no. 83, reprod.; Colnaghi to Paul J. Sachs.

BIBLIOGRAPHY: Mongan-Sachs, no. 468, fig. 240.
Roger A. d'Hulst and Horst Vey, *Antoon van Dyck, Tekeningen en olieverfschetsen*, Antwerp, 1960, p. 146.
Horst Vey, *Die Zeichnungen Anton van Dycks*, Brussels, 1962, 2 vols., I, pp. 39-40 and pl. I as "attributed to."

REMBRANDT VAN RIJN

Leyden 1606–Amsterdam 1669

22   A Woman Ill in Bed with a Child

Reed pen and bistre washed with bistre; green-grey wash added later, probably by an eighteenth-century hand. 7¼ x 9¼ in. (185 x 235 mm.)
Inscribed by a later hand: Rembrandt   1961.151

Benesch identified the woman as Rembrandt's wife, Saskia, playing with their son, Rumbartus, and on the basis of this concluded "that the drawing was not done before 1636." However, Dr. Van Eegher's archival research established that Rumbartus only lived two months (December 15, 1634-February 15, 1635) and since the child here is clearly older than two months, this attractive idea must be discarded. Judging upon the basis of style, the drawing is dated best in the late 1630's. The candle on the chair at the left, the layers of shade which transform the wicker chair into an open door leading into an illuminated room, and other chiaroscuro effects are additions of a later date. In the Hofstede de Groot Bequest, Rijksprentenkabinet, Amsterdam, there is a drawing of a similar subject and interior (Benesch 404).

PROVENANCE: Nathaniel Hone (Lugt 2793 recto); Marsden J. Perry (Lugt 1880 verso); Duveen to Paul J. Sachs, 1924.

BIBLIOGRAPHY: Mongan-Sachs, no. 522, fig. 268.
Tietze, 1947, p. 132, no. 66, reprod.
Otto Benesch, *The Drawings of Rembrandt,* London, 1954, II, no. 413, fig. 464.
I. H. van Eeghen, "De Kinderen van Rembrandt en Saskia," *Amstelodamum, Maandblad voor de Kennis van Amsterdam,* XLIII, 1956, pp. 144-146.
American Artist, March, 1963, reprod. without text, p. 22.

EXHIBITIONS: Worcester, Art Museum, Fiftieth Anniversary Exhibition of the Art of Europe, 1948, no. 9.
Cambridge, Fogg Art Museum, An Exhibition of Dutch and Flemish Drawings and Watercolors, 1954, no. 47.
New York, Pierpont Morgan Library and Cambridge, Fogg Art Museum, Rembrandt Drawings from American Collections, 1960, no. 33, pl. 28.

REMBRANDT VAN RIJN

Leyden 1606–Amsterdam 1669

23 Three Studies of a Child and One of an Old Woman

Quill pen and bistre wash, with slight retouches of grey-black (oxidized white) wash in the hair, on white paper. 8⅜ x 6¼ in. (214 x 160 mm.)

1949.4

Although the drawing is generally accepted as by Rembrandt himself, Benesch considers it an attributed work, or one by a gifted early pupil such as Lievens or Backer. He would date it in the early 1640's. Jakob Rosenberg, however, accepts it and associates it with Rembrandt's style of 1634-36. It seems possible (when one compares the quality of the pen line in the profile head of the woman with the strong hatchings in the washes beside the little girl's head) that Rembrandt returned, in the early forties, to an early drawing, as he frequently did, to rework the figures and enrich the plastic values of the heads.

PROVENANCE: Thomas Dimsdale (on verso, Lugt 2426); Marsden J. Perry (on verso, Lugt 1880); Duveen to Paul J. Sachs.

BIBLIOGRAPHY: Mongan-Sachs, no. 524, fig. 271.
American Artist, xv, no. 1, January, 1951, reprod. cover, noted p. 12.
Otto Benesch, The Drawings of Rembrandt, London, 1954, II, no. A10, fig. 581.
J. A. van Regteren Altena, Oud Holland, LXX, 1955, p. 120.
Jakob Rosenberg, Review of Benesch's Rembrandt, Art Bulletin, XXVIII, 1956, pp. 69-70.
W. Sumowski, "Bemerkungen zu Otto Beneschs corpus der Rembrandt Zeichnungen I," Wissenschaftliche Zeichschrift der Humboldt-Universität zu Berlin, Gesellschafts-und-sprach-wissenschaftliche Reihe, VI, 1956-57, p. 261.
Watrous, 1957, detail reprod. p. 49.

EXHIBITIONS: New York, Pierpont Morgan Library, and Cambridge, Fogg Art Museum, 1960, Rembrandt Drawings in American Collections, no. 21, pl. 17.

WENCESLAUS HOLLAR   Prague 1607–London 1677

24   A View of the Shore with Boats

Pen and ink with grey wash on white paper. 1¾ x 11⅞ in. (43 x 302 mm.)   1965.344

The drawing probably represents a Netherlands shore. However, Hollar traveled and drew so constantly and in such a number of countries, it is impossible to be sure. He accompanied Thomas Howard, the First Earl of Arundel, as recording artist when Howard journeyed up the Rhine and down the Danube in 1637 on his way to the Imperial Court. The views made on that journey—many are preserved at Chatsworth and in the British Museum—have, like the views of London and of Tangiers, the place names written at the top by the artist. It is possible that this drawing once had such an inscription and that the top of the drawing has been cropped. There are several landscape drawings that are of approximately this width but they are generally somewhat higher, like the British Museum's *View of Whitehall,* which measures 3⅞ x 11⅝ inches against the 1¾ x 11⅞ inches of this drawing. Hollar was again in the Lowlands in 1644 when, sharing the ill-fortunes of the Royalists, he escaped to Antwerp.

PROVENANCE: Keppel to Paul J. Sachs.

BIBLIOGRAPHY: Mongan-Sachs, no. 400, fig. 206.

JAN VAN GOYEN Leyden 1596–The Hague 1656

25 On the Seashore

Black chalk with grey wash on white paper. 4¾ x 7⅞ in. (120 x 195 mm.)
Watermark: Shield with a horn, with the letters MG below.
Signed and dated at lower left: VG 1652   1965.204

Dr. Hans Ulrich Beck of Munich is currently preparing a new catalogue-raisonné of Van Goyen's *oeuvre*. In a letter (December 14, 1964) he wrote that he believed the drawing was in a sale at Amsterdam, November 6, 1912, no. 108. It was bought by Gutekunst. This information seems confirmed by a pen notation on the back of the original frame "Bought in 1912." There is a copy of the drawing in the Print Room of the Rijksmuseum, Amsterdam, Inventory A3406 (Dr. Beck, same letter as above).

PROVENANCE: Keppel to Paul J. Sachs.

BIBLIOGRAPHY: Mongan-Sachs, no. 507, fig. 260.

PETER LELY   Soest, Westphalia 1618–London 1680

26 Two Poor Knights of Windsor

Black chalk heightened with white chalk (now largely effaced) on blue-grey paper. $19\frac{5}{16}$ x $13\frac{13}{16}$ in. (491 x 350 mm.)   1965.185

The drawing is one of a series of which at least thirty are now known. Sixteen are in the British Museum, the others in various public and private collections in Europe and America (see British Museum Catalogue, p. 409). Several of the British Museum drawings have been reworked "with oil-charcoal," a fate the Sachs drawing has happily escaped. It is not known for what purpose they were made, but it has been suggested that they were preliminary studies for a wall decoration for the Banqueting House at Whitehall, originally planned by Van Dyck. Lely owned Van Dyck's original oil sketch for a Garter Procession. Edward Croft-Murray and Paul Hulton (see below) also refer to a description of 1767 of a gallery at Burford House (the Duke of St. Albans) where there were represented the Knights of the Garter, all whole lengths done by Van Dyck and Sir Peter Lely. These pictures have disappeared. All the figures in the known drawings are connected with the ceremonies of the Order of the Garter on St. George's Day, April 23. Because of certain personages represented, the drawings must have been made between 1663 and 1671. The drawings were not in the vast and important sale of Lely's drawings after his death. The Poor Knights of Windsor were soldiers without fortune who had served the king, were pensioned by him, and lived in apartments at Windsor Castle.

PROVENANCE: De Leth, Amsterdam, anonymous sale, March 23, 1763, no. 16; Lord Northwick Sale, Sotheby's, London, July 6, 1921, no. 146; Colnaghi to Paul J. Sachs, 1922.

BIBLIOGRAPHY: Michel Benisovich, "Two Drawings by Peter Lely," *Burlington Magazine,* xci, March, 1959, pp. 77-81.
John Woodward, *Tudor and Stuart Drawings,* London, 1951, p. 49.
Edward Croft-Murray and Paul Hulton, *Catalogue of British Drawings* i, *Sixteenth and Seventeenth Centuries,* British Museum, London, 1960, p. 409.

WILLEM VAN DE VELDE,
the Younger   Amsterdam 1633–Greenwich 1707

27   A.   Two Men-of-War at Anchor
with three small boats   1965.216

B.   Seascape with Three Men-of-War,
a galliot, and several small boats   1965.215

Pen and bistre ink with India ink wash over graphite pencil underdraw-
ing. 3⅜ x 8½ in. (100 x 216 mm.)
Signed: W.V.V J (at the lower right in A; at the lower left in B)

PROVENANCE: A.   W. Esdaile (Lugt 2617), who wrote on the reverse in the
               lower left corner "1835 W E 168x" and added towards the cen-
               ter, "W. Van der Velde Jun"; C. S. Bale (Lugt 640); J. P.
               Heseltine; Keppel to Paul J. Sachs, 1913.

               B.   J. Harman; Samuel Woodburn; C. S. Bale; J. P. Heseltine
               (Lugt 1507, stamped on old mat); Keppel to Paul J. Sachs, 1913.

The drawings seem in style and size to be a pair, but the horizon line
is not at the same height, nor, as their provenance shows, have they always been together. From 1677 to 1685 Willem the Younger was em-
ployed by Charles II in England. After Charles's death, James II pensioned him. In 1686 he visited Amsterdam. These drawings were
probably made at that time, for the ships are flying Dutch flags. M. S.
Robinson (*Van de Velde Drawings in the National Maritime Museum*
[Greenwich], Cambridge, 1958, p. 23) has written: "To the period of
the Younger's visit to Holland in 1686 belong a number of sketches in
pen and brown ink with light grey wash mostly portraits of ships and
yachts. This group is distinguishable from the drawings of about 1700
by the more modest use of the pen, rather as a strengthening to the wash
instead of the wash being used to accentuate and fill out the pen-work."

BIBLIOGRAPHY: Mongan-Sachs, nos. 537, 536; figs. 278, 277.

ANTOINE WATTEAU

Valenciennes 1684–
Nogent-sur-Marne 1721

28 Six Studies of Heads

Natural red chalk, fabricated black chalk, heightened with white chalk
on chamois-colored paper. 8¾ x 8½ in. (222 x 217 mm.)   1965.336

Watteau filled his notebooks with studies of all kinds, copies from the
old masters, nude figures, heads, hands, feet, soldiers, actors, children,
animals and landscapes. He turned to these when he was ready to make
a painting and chose from the repertory of his sketchbooks what he
needed for his contemplated composition. The boy in the straw hat on
this page stands behind the two seated children in the painting, formerly at Potsdam, *Iris, c'est de bonne heure avoir l'air à la danse,* a
painting bought by Frederick II. The drawing for the head of the woman
appears again in a sheet of studies in the Louvre (Parker-Mathey, no.
720). This drawing, which shows Watteau at the peak of his powers,
probably was made about 1717-18.

PROVENANCE: Ivor Spencer Churchill; Durlacher(?) to Paul J. Sachs, Decem-
                ber 22, 1922.

BIBLIOGRAPHY: Mongan-Sachs, no. 641, fig. 325.
                Hélène Adhémar, *Watteau, sa vie—son oeuvre,* Paris, 1950, p.
                230.
                K. T. Parker and Jacques Mathey, *Antoine Watteau—son oeuvre
                dessiné,* 2 vols. Paris, 1957, II, p. 334, no. 712.

EXHIBITIONS: Rotterdam, Paris, New York, 1958-59, no. 91 (reprod. in color on
                cover).
                Baltimore, Museum of Art, 1959, Age of Elegance, the Rococo
                and its Effect, no. 78.

FRANÇOIS BOUCHER   Paris 1703–Paris 1770

29 Reclining Nude

Natural red chalk on chamois-colored paper. $12\frac{7}{16}$ x $16\frac{3}{8}$ in. (315 x 415 mm.)
Inscribed in ink at lower center: fr. Boucher   1965.235

The drawing is a preliminary study for a painting, *Venus and Mercury Instructing Cupid,* one of a series of over-door decorations which Boucher painted for the hôtel of Comte de Langonnay in the rue de Varennes. The painting, signed and dated 1738, is now in the Los Angeles County Museum. The drawing, with its rich and rhythmical line, is one of the most assured and graceful of Boucher's many drawings of the nude. In its pose and elegance and in the accents, especially those of the profile and the dimpled hands, there is still discernible Boucher's debt to Watteau.

PROVENANCE: Alphonse Kann Sale, Georges Petit Gallery, Paris, December 6-8, 1920, no. 74; Durlacher Brothers; gift of John Nicholas Brown to Paul J. Sachs, 1927.

BIBLIOGRAPHY: Mongan-Sachs, no. 596, fig. 305.
Sachs, 1951, pp. 88-90.

CLODION, Claude Michel called

Nancy 1738–Paris 1814

30 A Reclining Bacchante Holding a Vase

Black and white chalk on grey paper. 7⅛ x 11½ in. (181 x 292 mm.)

1965.243

Clodion, the most gifted of a family of decorator-sculptors, was a prolific artist. Vases, bas-reliefs, plaquettes, above all terra cotta statuettes came from his hand. Many survive so that his style is not unfamiliar, but although a portfolio of drawings was listed in the inventory of his possessions made after his death, his drawings are rare. His work, in its feminine grace and delicacy, is a plastic equivalent of Boucher's painting. As one would expect of a sculptor, in his drawings the movement is in three dimensions, circling constantly through the figure.

PROVENANCE: Alphonse Kann to Paul J. Sachs, 1920.

BIBLIOGRAPHY: Mongan-Sachs, no. 600, fig. 306.
Bouchet and Jaccottet, *Le dessin français au XVIIIme siècle,* Lausanne, 1952, p. 174, reprod. p. 115.

EXHIBITIONS: Rotterdam, Paris, New York, 1958-59, no. 40, pl. 84.

JEAN-BAPTISTE GREUZE   Tournus 1725–
Paris 1805

31 A Kneeling Youth with Outstretched Arms

Fabricated red chalk on white paper. 14¼ x 11¾ in. (362 x 299 mm.)

1965.291

Edgar Munhall was the first to notice that the drawing is a preparatory study for Greuze's frontispiece to Mme. Benoit's moralizing tale *Sophronie*. Greuze's design for that little-known illustration was executed in 1768. It was engraved by Moreau le Jeune and published a year later. In the printed version, as one would expect, the figure appears in reverse to the young man in the sketch. The drawing is, as Mr. Munhall points out, much livelier and more expressive than the engraving. Greuze had not exhibited in the Salon of 1767; therefore, his incursion into the field of illustration may have been an attempt to keep his name before the public. He made another illustration the following year for de Souvigny's *La Rosière* or *La Fête de Salency*. His third and last venture into book illustration was a drawing made for the Baskerville edition of Ariosto's *Orlando furioso* of 1773 (Martin, no. 409).

PROVENANCE: Georges Bourgarel; Bourgarel Sale, Paris, Hôtel Drouot, June 15-16, 1922, no. 96; Richard Owen to Paul J. Sachs, 1927.

BIBLIOGRAPHY: J. Martin, *Catalogue raisonné, Jean Baptiste Greuze,* Paris, 1905, p. 28, no. 408.
Mongan-Sachs, no. 624, fig. 313.
Edgar Munhall, "Greuze's Frontispiece for 'Sophronie,'" *Gazette des Beaux-Arts,* LVIII, 1961, pp. 237-242.

EXHIBITIONS: Detroit, 1951, no. 20.
Baltimore, Museum of Art, 1959, The Age of Elegance, the Rococo and its Effect, no. 56, reprod. p. 50.

JEAN-HONORE FRAGONARD

Grasse 1732–Paris 1806

32   A Woman Standing with Hand on Hip

Fabricated red chalk on white paper. 15¾ x 9¾ in. (381 x 247 mm.)

1965.276

According to Ananoff the drawing was shown in 1875 with the title *Study of a young woman in a satin dress*. A counterproof of the drawing is in the Czartoryski Museum, Cracow. The drawing is said to represent Fragonard's sister-in-law and assistant, Marguerite Gérard.

PROVENANCE: Thomas Dimsdale (Lugt 2426); William Mayor (Lugt 2799), sold in London in 1875; J. P. Heseltine; Guiraud Brothers, Paris; Wildenstein to Paul J. Sachs, May, 1919.

BIBLIOGRAPHY: Mongan-Sachs, no. 603, fig. 309.
Tietzé, 1947, p. 208.
Watrous, p. 122.
Gérard Bauër, *Dessins français du Dixhuitième Siècle: La figure humaine,* Paris, 1959, pl. 30.
S. Sawicka, *Wystawa Rysunkow Francuskich Ze Zbiorow Amerykanskich,* xxi, 1959, pp. 364-366 (but captions of drawing and counterproof have accidentally been reversed).
Alexandre Ananoff, *L'Oeuvre Dessiné de Jean-Honoré Fragonard,* Paris, 1963, II, p. 69, no. 726, fig. 212.

EXHIBITIONS: San Francisco, 1940, no. 36, p. 78, reprod.
Paris, Rotterdam, New York, 1958, no. 48, pl. 73.
Baltimore, Museum of Art, 1959, Age of Elegance, The Rococo and its Effect, no. 49.
New York, Knoedler's, 1959, Great Master Drawings of Seven Centuries, pp. 63-64.

GIOVANNI BATTISTA TIEPOLO

Venice 1696–Madrid 1770

33 The Holy Family Enthroned, with St. Sebastian, St. Catherine of Alexandria, and St. Francis (?)

Brush and bistre wash over black chalk on white paper. 17 x 11⅞ in.
(432 x 302 mm.)   1965.417

The drawing probably dates from the early 1740's when Tiepolo was
at the height of his powers, loaded with commissions both sacred and
profane, his never-idle hand inventing an endless variety of scenes and
figures. His drawings have brilliance, elegance, ease and economy that
have remained unmatched. In this drawing there are echoes of Bellini
and Veronese, but more movement in the figures and a more spirited
play of light and shadow than the sixteenth century would have known.
There are two other variants of the drawing known, one in Berlin
(reprod. von Hadeln, *Die Handzeichnungen von G. B. Tiepolo,* Munich, 1927, I, pl. 42); the other was in the collection of Paul Wallraf
(formerly Orloff, see below). There is a fourth related drawing in the
Uffizi and a fifth in the de Courcelles Collection, Paris.

PROVENANCE: Prince Alexis Orloff Sale, Georges Petit Gallery, Paris, April 29-
30, 1920, no. 135, reprod.; Paul Drey to Paul J. Sachs, 1928.

BIBLIOGRAPHY: Mongan-Sachs, no. 346, fig. 171.
Helen Comstock, "Eighteenth-Century Italian Figure Drawings
at the Fogg Art Museum," *Connoisseur,* cxxxv, May, 1955, pp.
274-280, fig. 1.

EXHIBITIONS: Oberlin College, Allen Memorial Museum, 1951, Master Draw-
ings of the 18th Century in France and Italy, no. 18, reprod.
Catalogue published as Vol. viii, no. 2, of *Allen Memorial Art
Museum Bulletin.*

GIOVANNI BATTISTA TIEPOLO

Venice 1696–Madrid 1770

34   The Rest on the Flight

Pen and bistre over traces of black chalk on white paper. 16⅞ x 11⅜ in.
(430 x 290 mm.)   1965.418

Like the preceding drawing, this too was probably made in the early
1740's and also, like the preceding, it is a drawing of which many variants
exist, for the theme of the Flight into Egypt was a favorite one of Tiepolo's. Since the Second World War a number of them have passed into
American collections.

PROVENANCE: Prince Alexis Orloff Sale, Georges Petit Gallery, Paris, April 29-
                30, 1920, no. 79, reprod.; Paul J. Sachs.

BIBLIOGRAPHY: Mongan-Sachs, no. 347, fig. 172.
                Sachs, 1951, p. 44, pl. 29.
                Helen Comstock, "Eighteenth-Century Italian Figure Drawings
                at the Fogg Art Museum," *Connoisseur,* cxxv, May, 1955, pp.
                274-80, fig. 4.
                Jakob Rosenberg, "The Problem of Quality in Old Master Draw-
                ings," *Allen Memorial Art Museum Bulletin,* Oberlin, viii, no.
                2, Winter 1951, p. 46, fig. 10a.

GIOVANNI BATTISTA PIRANESI

Near Venice 1720–Rome 1778

35 Roman Ruins

Quill and reed(?) pen and iron-gall ink on white paper. 10½ x 14¾ in.
(267 x 375 mm.)   1965.409

The drawing is similar in style to some other drawings of Piranesi's early
years in Rome, that is to those made between 1745-50. The echoes of his
Venetian training have not yet faded. Although the drawing is probably
not for a stage set, it is not unlike the few drawings which can be con-
sidered as designs for the theater. Elements from Roman antiquity are
combined to make a fanciful but powerful scene.

PROVENANCE: Alphonse Kann Sale, American Art Association, New York,
               January 7, 1930, no. 44. Bought at the sale by Paul J. Sachs.

BIBLIOGRAPHY: Mongan-Sachs, no. 343, fig. 168.
               Thomas Hylton, *The Drawings of Giovanni Battista Piranesi*,
               London and New York, 1954, p. 44, no. 28.

EXHIBITIONS: Boston, Museum of Fine Arts, 1945, A Thousand Years of Land-
               scape East and West.
               Oberlin, Allen Memorial Museum, 1951, Master Drawings of the
               Eighteenth Century in France and Italy, no. 15.

FRANCESCO GUARDI   Venice 1712–Venice 1793

36   A View of the Giudecca with the Redentore at the Left

Pen and light-brown wash with annotations for color and tone. 3¾ x 12¼ in. (95 x 312 mm.)
Verso: Sketches of Venetian houses in red chalk.   1965.384

The view represents the left half of a wide panorama of the Bacino di San Marco. The right half, which is in the National Gallery of Canada, Ottawa, shows the Salute, the Dogana and the entrance to the Grand Canal. Apparently the Sachs drawing at one time had, like the Ottawa drawing, an empty expanse of water in the foreground. J. Byam Shaw suggests that the two drawings and a third, which carried the view of the end of the Giudecca at the left, were made by Guardi from a boat in the Bacino and used by him in preparing somewhat later the large (13¾ x 26⅝ in.) and extensive panorama in the collection of Lady Catherine Ashburnham, Battle, Sussex. The Ottawa drawing was dated in the 1965 Guardi Exhibition "after 1775," a date that should hold as well for the Sachs drawing.

PROVENANCE: Langton Douglas to Paul J. Sachs.

BIBLIOGRAPHY: Mongan-Sachs, no. 322, fig. 160.
James Byam Shaw, *The Drawings of Francesco Guardi,* London, 1951, pp. 63-64.

EXHIBITIONS: Venice, Palazzo Grassi, 1965, Mostra dei Guardi, Catalogo dei disegni, no. 57, reprod.

PIERRE-PAUL PRUD'HON   Cluny 1758–
Paris 1823

40   Nymph Teased by Cupids

Verso: Academic Study of a Male Nude
Black and white chalk and wash on blue paper, squared for enlargement.
21$\frac{1}{16}$ x 16$\frac{3}{8}$ in. (535 x 415 mm.)   1965.326

In addition to this drawing and the oil sketch in the Louvre (758A), M. Guiffrey lists seven other studies all made in preparation for the painting which Constance Meyer, Prud'hon's pupil, exhibited in the Salon of 1812. The academic sketch of a male nude recently uncovered on the verso of the sheet is one of many done by Prud'hon in his later years when he made studies after the model in the studio of another pupil, Trezel. Only rarely do these studies relate to his paintings or prints.

PROVENANCE: De Boisfremont (Lugt 353); Deniere; Jacques De Bryas; Stettiner; Baron Maurice de Rothschild; Wildenstein to Paul J. Sachs, December, 1922.

BIBLIOGRAPHY: Mongan-Sachs, no. 634, fig. 320.

EXHIBITIONS: Detroit, 1951, no. 24, reprod.

THÉODORE GÉRICAULT
Rouen 1791–Paris
1824

41 An Italian Landscape

Pen with brown ink, blue and brown wash over black chalk on white
paper. 9⅛ x 8⅛ in. (232 x 207 mm.)   1965.287

We are keeping the title originally given to the drawing in spite of the
reappearance, after a hundred years, of the painting to which it is so
clearly related. That painting, entitled *Fisherman at Sunset,* Huntington
Hartford Gallery of Modern Art, New York, turned up in Europe in
1959 (Sale, Charpentier Gallery, Paris, December 3, 1959, no. 52). Spe-
cialists then recalled Clément's reference to such a scene. A sheet of three
sketches formerly in the collection of Pierre Dubaut and a sheet of studies
with six horizontal rows of studies of men pulling a boat (formerly in an
album that belonged to David d'Angers, present whereabouts unknown)
are, like our drawing, indubitably related to the painting. Clément wrote
that such a landscape painting hung in Géricault's studio while he was at
work on the *Raft of the Medusa.* The links are strong between the figure
studies for the *Raft,* the Fualdès series, and the detail studies of the
straining figures who appear also in the Sachs drawing, so there seems
reason to place the date of the Sachs drawing somewhat later than we
did before, that is to consider it a work of about 1817-18.

PROVENANCE: Mathey; Duc de Trévise Sale, Charpentier Gallery, Paris, May
              19, 1938, no. 18. (The Charpentier catalogue speaks of a signa-
              ture "en partie effacée." We can find no evidence of a signa-
              ture.) Maurice Gobin to Paul J. Sachs, August, 1938.

BIBLIOGRAPHY: Mongan-Sachs, no. 692, fig. 363.
              Klaus Berger, *Géricault's Drawings and Watercolors,* New York,
              1946, no. 1.
              Lorenz Eitner, "Two Rediscovered Landscapes by Géricault,"
              Art Bulletin, xxxvi, June, 1954, p. 135, fig. 9.
              Max Huggler, "Two Unknown Landscapes by Géricault," *Bur-
              lington Magazine,* xcvi, August, 1954, p. 234.
              Robert Lebel, "Géricault, Ses Ambitions monumentales et
              l'inspiration italienne," *L'Arte,* xxv, 1960, p. 329.

EXHIBITIONS: Detroit, 1951, no. 43, reprod.

THÉODORE GÉRICAULT   Rouen 1791–Paris
1824

42   Negro Soldier Holding a Lance

Brush with brown ink and grey wash over graphite pencil. $13\frac{3}{16}$ x $9\frac{13}{16}$
in. (335 x 249 mm.)   1965.285

Joseph, a familiar model in the Paris ateliers of the time, posed for Géricault wearing a costume that the artist, who had a variety of North Afri-
can costumes in his studio, assembled for him. The exotic clothing is but
the point of departure for the dramatic presentation, the bold chiaroscuro
and the strong sense of physical power held in equilibrium on the verge
of action. Although not dated, the drawing was undoubtedly made not
between 1820-24 when Clément dated it, but ca. 1817-18 when Géricault
was at work on the *Raft of the Medusa,* using Joseph often as a model.

PROVENANCE: De l'Aage; Marmontel; A. Beurdeley; Scott and Fowles to Paul J.
Sachs.

BIBLIOGRAPHY: Mongan-Sachs, no. 694, fig. 365.
Klaus Berger, *Géricault Drawings and Watercolors,* New York,
1946, p. 33, pl. 46.
Sachs, 1951, p. 96, pl. 57.
Klaus Berger, *Géricault and His Work,* trans. W. Ames, Law-
rence, Kansas, 1955, p. 86, no. 82, reprod.
Carl Georg Heise, *Grosse Zeichner Des XIX Jahrhunderts,* Ber-
lin, 1959, p. 84, no. 64.
F. H. Lem, "La thème du negre dans l'oeuvre de Géricault,"
L'Arte, January-June, 1962, p. 29.
Antonio del Guercio, *Géricault,* Milan, 1963, pp. 86, 151, pl. 89.

EXHIBITIONS: San Francisco, 1947, no. 25, reprod. p. 25.
Paris, 1955, no. 76, pl. 11.
Rotterdam, Paris, New York, 1958-59, no. 123, pl. 112.

JEAN-AUGUSTE-DOMINIQUE
INGRES

Montauban 1780–Paris 1867

43   Portrait of Madame Hayard, née Jeanne Suzanne Allion

Graphite pencil on white paper. 10½ x 7$\frac{1}{16}$ in. (267 x 180 mm.)
Signed at the lower right: Ingres   1965.298

The Hayard family were friends of Ingres in Rome. He drew this ex-
quisite portrait about 1812. Three years later he made two other drawings of the Hayard family, Mme. Hayard with her daughter, Caroline,
which came to the Fogg Museum in the Winthrop Bequest in 1943, and
Monsieur Hayard with their elder daughter Marguerite (Private Collection). Marguerite became Mme. Félix Duban. Ingres drew her portrait again in 1841, an indication that the friendship remained strong.
The Sachs drawing passed from Marguerite to Caroline, who became
Mme. Flachéron.

PROVENANCE: Mme. Felix Duban (née Hayard); Mme. Flachéron; Georges
                Bernheim; John Levy Gallery to Paul J. Sachs, January, 1922.

BIBLIOGRAPHY: Mongan-Sachs, no. 699, fig. 370.
                Jean Alazard, *Ingres et l'Ingrisme,* Paris, 1950, p. 51, pl. XXII.
                Daniel Ternois, *Les dessins d'Ingres au Musée de Montauban,*
                1959, see no. 72.
                Roberta M. Capers and Jerrold Maddox, *Images and Imagina-
                tion, An Introduction to Art,* New York, 1965, p. 265, fig. 10-
                11.

EXHIBITIONS: San Francisco, 1947, no. 2.
                Rotterdam, Paris, New York, 1958-59, no. 129, pl. 105.
                Berkeley, University of California, 1960, Art from Ingres to
                Pollock, p. 58.
                New York, Paul Rosenberg Gallery, 1961, Ingres in American
                Collections, no. 11.

JEAN-AUGUSTE-DOMINIQUE INGRES

Montauban 1780–Paris 1867

44 A Crouching Nude Youth Reaching for a Stone; Separate Study of Arm

Graphite pencil and black crayon with touches of red crayon in the separate arm, on white paper, squared. On the reverse in Ingres' hand: Cavalier port (*sic*) le casque, tireur porte enseigne (a reference to other figures in the painting). 15⅜ x 19½ in. (390 x 495 mm.)
Signed at lower left (covered by mat): Ingr   1965.296

A study for the painting *The Martyrdom of St. Symphorien,* commissioned by the government in 1826 at the request of the Bishop of Autun, who wished a replacement for the Fra Bartolommeo altarpiece that had been taken to Paris during the Revolution. The Bishop selected the subject, choosing a local martyr. Ingres struggled with the painting. He did not finish it until 1834. When it was then severely criticized, Ingres requested and received the post of Director of the French Academy in Rome. There are more than two hundred and fifty studies for the painting at Montauban. There is another study for the *Crouching Youth* in the Bonnat Museum, Bayonne, and a very fine page, with drawings on both sides, in the Nelson Gallery, Kansas City. The Fogg received in the Winthrop Bequest two oil sketches for the painting and a later working drawing which is squared, perhaps for the engraver.

PROVENANCE: Flameng Sale, Georges Petit Gallery, March 26-27, 1919, no. 124; Maurice Le Garrec to Paul J. Sachs.

BIBLIOGRAPHY: Mongan-Sachs, no. 702, fig. 373.
                Jean Alazard, *Ingres et l'Ingrisme,* Paris, 1950, pl. LXV.

EXHIBITIONS: Rotterdam, Paris, New York, 1958-59, no. 132, pl. 110.
                New York, Paul Rosenberg Gallery, 1961, Ingres in American Collections, no. 35.
                Vancouver, Art Gallery, 1964, The Nude in Art, no. 55.

JEAN-AUGUSTE-DOMINIQUE
INGRES
Montauban 1780–Paris 1867

45 Portrait of Madame d'Haussonville

Graphite pencil on white paper, squared for enlargement. $9\frac{1}{4}$ x $11\frac{5}{16}$ in.
(235 x 295 mm.)
Signed at lower left: Ing

1965.294

Mme. d'Haussonville (1818-82), born Louise de Broglie, was the grand-daughter of Mme. de Staël and the great-granddaughter of Joseph Necker. In 1836 she married the Vicomte Othenin d'Haussonville, then Secretary to Ambassador Alquier, later Deputy, Senator, historian, and member of the French Academy. In Rome as a young man, Ingres had been commissioned by Alquier, then the Ambassador to the Holy See, to paint the now-famous *Portrait of Mme. Devauçay*. In 1842 Ingres accepted the commission to paint the portrait of the lively Vicomtesse. He did a preliminary oil sketch that year, but he abandoned his first plan. It was four years, after many sketches and sittings, trials and tempers, before the portrait, now in the Frick Collection, was brought to a triumphant finish. In this study the pose is very close to that of the painted portrait, but there is a certain informality, in both dress and mood, that brings her closer to the observer.

PROVENANCE: A. Beurdeley Sale, Georges Petit Gallery, Paris, December 2, 1920, no. 242; Wildenstein to Paul J. Sachs, April 18, 1927.

BIBLIOGRAPHY: Mongan-Sachs, no. 704, fig. 375.
Jean Alazard, *Ingres et l'Ingrisme,* Paris, 1950, pl. LXXIX.
Daniel Ternois, *Les dessins d'Ingres au Musée de Montauban, Les Portraits,* Inventaire général des dessins de Musées de Province, 1959, above no. 64.

EXHIBITIONS: Rotterdam, Paris, New York, 1958-59, no. 135, pl. 108.
New York, Paul Rosenberg Gallery, 1961, Ingres in American Collections, no. 55.

JEAN-AUGUSTE-DOMINIQUE INGRES

Montauban 1780–Paris 1867

46 Study for Portrait of Madame d'Haussonville

Black crayon over pencil on white paper. 14 x 8 in. (365 x 204 mm.)
At the right near the sleeve, in Ingres' handwriting: plus de movement;
below in fireplace opening: grand foyer de Carmin   1965.295

In this study, Mme. d'Haussonville is in the exact pose, even the dress of
the finished painting, although here she wears a scarf over her shoulders
that is later abandoned. Other studies of this pose are in the museum at
Montauban, the British Museum, and the Frick Collection.

PROVENANCE: M. Ernst May; Alphonse Kann to Paul J. Sachs, February, 1920.

BIBLIOGRAPHY: Mongan-Sachs, no. 705, fig. 376.
Jean Alazard, *Ingres et l'Ingrisme,* Paris, 1950, pl. LXXVIII.
Arthur Millier, *The Drawings of Ingres,* Los Angeles, 1955, pl. 38.
Jakob Rosenberg, 1959, p. xxii.
Daniel Ternois, *Les dessins d'Ingres au Musée de Montauban,*
Les Portraits, Inventaire général des dessins de Musées de
Province, 1959, above no. 64.

EXHIBITIONS: New York, Paul Rosenberg Gallery, 1961, Ingres in American
Collections, no. 56.

plus de mouvement

grand foyer de
lumière

EUGÈNE DELACROIX

Charenton 1798–Paris 1863

47 Portrait of Frédéric Villot (1809-1875)

Dark grey and black chalk, with some graphite pencil accents and extensive stumping, accented with very soft charcoal or black crayon on white Whatman paper. 13⅛ x 9⅜ in. (333 x 237 mm.)
Stamp of the Delacroix Sale, faint and upside down at lower right, clear at lower left.   1949.6

In 1832 Delacroix painted a portrait of Villot now in the National Museum, Prague (Venice Biennale, 1956, and Louvre Exposition, 1963, no. 151 bis). A year later he made a reduced copy which belonged to Villot's son. In 1838 he made another portrait described in the Louvre catalogue as "de face" and "inachevé." The Sachs drawing may be related to the latter; Villot is represented "de face" and as somewhat older than in the Prague portrait of 1832-33. The Sachs drawing also remained in Delacroix's studio until after the artist's death. Frédéric Villot, an intimate friend of Delacroix from the time that they both were young, was made Curator of Paintings at the Louvre on February 24, 1848. It was he who initiated a new hanging of the paintings, a more modern series of catalogues, and a scientific study of conservation and restoration. Yet, just when the friendship between artist and critic might have grown deeper, it suddenly cooled to superficial politeness. (Michel Florisoone, "La Mort d'une Amitié, Delacroix and Villot," *Archives de l'art français,* Nouvelle Periode, xxii, 1959, pp. 383-399).

PROVENANCE: Delacroix Sale, Paris, February 17-24, 1864; A. Robaut; J. F. Gigoux Sale, Paris, 1882; Théodore Duret; César M. de Hauke to Paul J. Sachs.

BIBLIOGRAPHY: Mongan-Sachs, no. 682, fig. 357.
Vincent Price, *Drawings of Delacroix,* Los Angeles, 1961.
Lee Johnson, *Delacroix,* An Exhibition arranged by the Arts Council, Edinburgh and London, 1964, p. 26, under no. 28.

EXHIBITIONS: San Francisco, 1947, no. 32, p. 29, reprod.
Detroit, 1951, no. 38, reprod.
Paris, 1955, no. 72, pl. 17.

EUGÈNE DELACROIX   Charenton 1798–Paris
1863

48   A Mounted Arab Attacking a Panther

Graphite pencil on white paper. 9½ x 8 in. (240 x 204 mm.)
Stamp of the Darcy Collection at lower right (Lugt 652f).   1965.268

Denys Darcy (1823-1904) was the author of the Delacroix tomb in Père
Lachaise Cemetery. Lugt supposes that at the time he designed the tomb
he was given a batch of Delacroix's drawings (the stamp is to be found
only on Delacroix drawings). His daughter inherited the drawings and
her daughter sold them (one hundred and sixty-five sheets) to Cailac,
the Paris dealer. In 1937 Maurice Gobin had a number of them, including
this one, which Paul J. Sachs then acquired.

René Huyghe (*Delacroix, ou le combat solitaire,* Paris, 1964, p. 496)
points out that the theme of struggle is fundamental in Delacroix,
whether between an animal and its prey, a wild beast against a wild
beast, a man against a man, or a man against a wild beast. Traditionally
the animal here has been called a panther, but it could as well be a
tiger. The Minneapolis catalogue points out that the Arab has his sword
in his left hand and suggests that Delacroix may have copied an engraving which reversed a painted composition.

PROVENANCE: Delacroix family to Darcy; Cailac; Maurice Gobin to Paul J.
Sachs, 1937.

BIBLIOGRAPHY: Mongan-Sachs, no. 683, fig. 356.
Vincent Price, *Drawings of Delacroix,* Los Angeles, 1961.
René Huyghe, editor, *L'art et l'homme,* Paris, 1961, III, p. 295,
no. 1035.

EXHIBITIONS: Rotterdam, Paris, New York, 1958-59, no. 116, pl. 131.
Minneapolis, University Gallery, and New York, Guggenheim
Museum, 1962, The Nineteenth Century: One Hundred
Twenty-five Master Drawings, no. 32, pl. 20, reprod. on cover.
Paris, Louvre, 1963, Eugène Delacroix, Exposition du Cen-
tenaire, no. 463.

JEAN-BAPTISTE-CAMILLE COROT

Paris 1796–Paris 1875

49 A View of Mount Soracte from Città Castellana

Pen and iron-gall ink over pencil on white paper. 11 x 16⅜ in. (280 x 415 mm.)
Inscribed in Corot's hands at lower right: Città Castellana 7bre 1827
Red stamp of the Giraud Sale at lower right.   1965.247

Corot sketched and painted Mount Soracte many times in the two successive summers of 1826 and 1827 when he went on trips into the countryside around Rome. Among the surviving drawings (Robaut lists more than twenty made at Città Castellana) there is none which surpasses this drawing in nobility of conception or vibrancy of atmosphere. A painting of 1827 from a slightly different viewpoint was acquired recently by the Ny Carlsberg Glyptotek (see reference below). Another belonged to Daubigny, a gift of the artist (Robaut, no. 125). Soracte, the mountain which rises majestically out of the Campagna north of Rome, also gave inspiration to Horace, Virgil and Byron.

PROVENANCE: Giraud Sale, Paris, February 9-13, 1886; Duc de Trévise Sale, Charpentier Gallery, Paris, May 19, 1938; Gobin to Paul J. Sachs, 1938.

BIBLIOGRAPHY: Mongan-Sachs, no. 650, fig. 328.
Shoolman and Slatkin, p. 138.
Sachs, 1951, p. 99 and pl. 60.
Watrous, p. 73.
Haavard Rostrup, "Den Guddmmelige Corot," *Meddefelser fra Ny Carlsberg Glyptotek,* 1960, p. 28.

EXHIBITIONS: Philadelphia, Museum of Art, 1946, Corot, no. 80, reprod.
San Francisco, 1947, no. 38, reprod. p. 31.
Philadelphia, Museum of Art, 1950-51, Masterpieces of Drawing, Diamond Jubilee Exhibition, no. 86, reprod.
Rotterdam, Paris, New York, 1958-59, no. 98, pl. 12a.
Chicago, Art Institute, 1960, Corot, no. 150.

Castle Eastlin ... 1809

JEAN-BAPTISTE-CAMILLE COROT

Paris 1796–Paris 1875

50   Henry Leroy as a Child

Graphite pencil on white paper. 10¾ x 9⅞ in. (275 x 250 mm.)
Inscribed lower right in pencil: Corot   1965.245

The identification of Henry Leroy (and the first name ends with the
English "y" not the French "i") was made in a letter signed "Laure
Henry Leroy, 2 Janvier 1914" which was on the reverse of the frame. We
have not found the full name in the Corot literature, but there seems to
be no reason to doubt its accuracy. Corot sketched the children of rela-
tives and friends many times. In the Mongan-Sachs catalogue we dated
the drawing about 1835. Further study has led us to believe, because of
its plastic incisive qualities and the manner in which the figure is de-
tached from its background, that it should be placed somewhat later,
perhaps as late as 1845-50, when he did the portraits of the children of
his former patron, Édouard Delalain (Robaut, nos. 595 and 596). For
Paul Sachs this was "a drawing in which there is a complete absence of
any calligraphic trick, a drawing which renders a mood miraculously."

PROVENANCE: Mme. Laure Henry Leroy; Mme. Moyse; Paul Rosenberg to
                 Paul J. Sachs, July 2, 1928.

BIBLIOGRAPHY: Mongan-Sachs, no. 652, fig. 330.
                 Tietze, 1947, no. 132.
                 Sachs, 1954, p. 24, pl. 18.
                 Carl Heise, *Grosse Zeichner Des XIX Jahrhunderts,* Berlin, 1959,
                 p. 88, fig. 68.

EXHIBITIONS: San Francisco, 1947, no. 39, reprod   p. 32.
                 Paris, 1955, no. 62, pl. 19.
                 Chicago, Art Institute, 1960, Corot, no. 162.
                 Berkeley, University of California, 1960. Art from Ingres to
                 Pollock, p. 56.

JEAN-FRANÇOIS MILLET

Gréville 1814–
Barbizon 1875

51 Portrait of Madame Alfred Sensier

Fabricated black chalk and colored chalks on white paper. 12¾ x 10 in.
(324 x 254 mm.)   1963.144

Mme. Sensier was the wife of the critic Sensier, who was Millet's devoted
admirer and biographer. He was Millet's landlord at Barbizon where
this drawing was probably made in the early 1850's. Sensier was chief
of the Bureau of Museums from 1848-50, after which he entered the Min-
istry of the Interior. He retired in 1873 and died in 1877.

PROVENANCE: Alfred Sensier; Mme. Duhamel (née Marguerite Sensier) to
                César M. de Hauke in 1938; to Paul J. Sachs the same year.

BIBLIOGRAPHY: Mongan-Sachs, no. 713, fig. 382.

EXHIBITIONS: San Francisco, 1947, no. 44.
                Rotterdam, Paris, New York, 1958-59, no. 138, pl. 146.

JEAN-FRANÇOIS MILLET

Gréville 1814–
Barbizon 1875

52 Marguerite Sensier as a Baby

Black and colored chalks on white paper. 10½ x 8 in. (268 x 203 mm.)

1965.311

Marguerite was the Sensier's only surviving child. After her father's death, she inherited his large collection of Millet drawings, prints and pastels. As Mme. Duhamel, she evicted Millet's widow from the Barbizon house where the painter and his family had lived for almost thirty years. In the Louvre there is a quick sketch from life (Louvre 10620) which shows a woman holding on her lap a baby in the same dress and position as in this drawing. One is led to conclude that Millet intended to make a portrait of Mme. Sensier holding Marguerite. (This drawing probably dates from ca. 1866.)

PROVENANCE: Alfred Sensier; Mme. Duhamel (née Marguerite Sensier); César M. de Hauke to Paul J. Sachs, 1947.

BIBLIOGRAPHY: Agnes Mongan, *One Hundred Master Drawings,* Cambridge, 1949, p. 166, reprod.

EXHIBITIONS: Detroit, 1951, no. 49.

HONORÉ DAUMIER   Marseilles 1808–Valmondois
1879

53   Two Lawyers Conversing

Black crayon, pen with carbon ink, watercolor washes in ochre, blue and grey and heightening in grey gouache. $10\frac{1}{16}$ x $6\frac{1}{2}$ in.   (255 x 165 mm.)
Signed at the lower left: h Daumier   1965.250

The drawing was undoubtedly made in the sixties when Daumier was at the height of his power. From that decade came many a satiric scene in which the pomposities and poses of lawyers were sometimes subtly and sometimes sharply lampooned by the artist.

PROVENANCE: A. Beurdeley; Maurice Gobin to Paul J. Sachs, 1922.

BIBLIOGRAPHY: Mongan-Sachs, no. 657, fig. 333.
Heinrich Schwarz, "Daumier: Last Great Illustrator," *Art News,* XLIV, no. 15 (Nov. 15, 1945), p. 20ff.

EXHIBITIONS: Detroit, Art Institute, 1951, no. 31, reprod.
Boston, Museum of Fine Arts, 1958, Honoré Daumier, no. 104.
London, Arts Council, 1961, Daumier; Paintings and Drawings, no. 205, pl. 34c.

ÉDOUARD MANET Paris 1832–Paris 1883

54 A Café Interior

Quill(?) pen and India ink on pale tan paper faded to reddish brown within the mat opening. 11⅝ x 15½ in. (295 x 396 mm.)
Signed and dated at the lower right: Manet/1869; and in pencil beneath the mat: E. Manet   1965.304

Two lithographs, both entitled *Le Café* (Marcel Guérin, *L'Oeuvre Gravé de Manet,* Paris, 1944, nos. 80 and 81), repeat the scene of the drawing but with some changes in the position of the figures and with the addition of mirror reflections in the left background. The lithograph measures 10½ x 13⅞, that part of the drawing revealed by the window of the mat, 8⅞ x 11⅝. A note on the back of the frame says that the drawing had once belonged to the art critic Castagnary and that Manet had represented himself in the drawing in the standing, bearded man, adding that there is little doubt that it was done in the Café Nouvelle Athènes. John Rewald (conversation), who doubts that Manet represented himself, believes that the Café is more probably the Café Guerbois, noting that Manet and his friends did not gather at the Nouvelle Athènes until about 1872. Alain de Leiris' *The Drawings of Edouard Manet* (Ph.D. thesis, Harvard, 1957, no. 230) notes that the bold pen line defines each object and also interprets the light, achieving through the latter a new kind of unity in the absence of a dramatic focus.

PROVENANCE: Castagnary; Scott and Fowles to Paul J. Sachs, 1919.

BIBLIOGRAPHY: Mongan-Sachs, no. 709, fig. 378.
Sachs, 1954, p. 10.

EXHIBITIONS: San Francisco, 1947, no. 73.
Minneapolis, University Gallery, and New York, Guggenheim Museum, 1962, The Nineteenth Century: One Hundred Twenty-five Master Drawings, no. 74, pl. 37.

EDGAR DEGAS   Paris 1834–Paris 1917

55   Study for Portrait of Madame Julie Burtin (Madame Jules Bertin?)

Hard and soft graphite pencils on white paper with touches of white chalk about her hair and face. 14¼ x 10¾ in. (361 x 272 mm.)
Watermark: A tree within a circle
Inscribed in the upper right in crayon in Degas' writing: Mme. Julie Burtin   1965.254

The drawing is a study for the portrait *Femme en robe noire,* in the collection of Jacques Lindon, New York (Lemoisne, no. 108). There is a separate study of the head in the Clark Art Institute, Williamstown, which is signed and dated in pencil at top right: Degas/1863, and at the bottom, annotated: Mme. Jules Bertin [*sic*]. The Bibliothèque Nationale has a sketchbook (Carnet 7) with studies of the hands. The date on the Clark drawing is probably also the date of the more complete Sachs drawing. Which reading is correct, that recorded on the Sachs drawing, which is clearly in the artist's own hand, or the annotation on the Clark drawing with the more common name "Bertin" is not yet known. In any event, the Sachs drawing is one of the most subtle and beautiful of the drawings which Degas made while still in his twenties. It shows clearly his debt to Ingres, and to the Quattrocento Italians whom he had studied assiduously in his early visits to Italy.

PROVENANCE: Second Degas Sale, Georges Petit Gallery, Paris, December 11-13, 1918, no. 347 (red stamp of the sale at the lower left corner); Mme. Demotte to Paul J. Sachs, July 3, 1928.

BIBLIOGRAPHY: Mongan-Sachs, no. 663, fig. 339.
Watrous, pp. 144-145.
Rosenberg, 1959, p. 108.
Jean Boggs, *Portraits by Degas,* Los Angeles, 1962, pl. 35.

EXHIBITIONS: San Francisco, 1947, no. 87.
Los Angeles, Art Museum, 1958, Degas, no. 13, reprod.
Rotterdam, Paris, New York, 1958-59, no. 160, pl. 155.

Mme Julie Burty

Degas

EDGAR DEGAS

Paris 1834–Paris 1917

56   Portrait Sketch of Édouard Manet

Graphite pencil on white paper. 14¼ x 9¹⁄₁₆ in. (363 x 230 mm.)

1965.261

Degas made several sketches of Édouard Manet in preparation for the three etched portraits of 1864 (Delteil, IX, 1919, nos. 14, 15, 16). This one and two others, which were in the same frame with it at the time of the Degas sales, were erroneously said to represent Édouard's brother Eugène. Three other studies are in the Metropolitan Museum (Havemeyer Collection) and two in the Rouart Collection, Paris.

PROVENANCE: Fourth Degas Sale, Georges Petit Gallery, Paris, July 3-4, 1919, no. 248A (red stamp of the sale at the lower left); Madame de Zayas to Paul J. Sachs.

BIBLIOGRAPHY: Mongan-Sachs, no. 666, fig. 342.

Degas

Fb 1902

EDGAR DEGAS

Paris 1834–Paris 1917

57   Study for the Portrait of Madame Hertel (La Dame aux Chrysanthèmes)

Graphite pencil on white paper. 14 x 9⅛ in. (355 x 234 mm.)
Signed and dated at the lower right: degas/1865   1965.253

The drawing is a study for the painting in the Metropolitan Museum best known as *La Dame aux Chrysanthèmes* (Lemoisne, no. 125). In the painting the vase of chrysanthemums occupies the central position. Mme. Hertel sits at the right. It was the first of the many paintings in which Degas placed the figure off the central axis, an idea which he may have borrowed from a Millet pastel in the collection of his great friends the Rouarts.

PROVENANCE: Paul Rosenberg to Paul J. Sachs.

BIBLIOGRAPHY: Mongan-Sachs, no. 667, fig. 343.
Tietze, 1947, no. 144.
British Broadcasting Company, *The Nature of Drawing,* London, 1959, p. 24, fig. 29.
Yujiro Shinoda, *Degas, Der Einzug des Japanischen in die französische Malerei* (Inaugural Dissertation), Cologne, 1957, p. 34.
Jaromír Pečírka, *Edgar Degas, Drawings,* London, 1963, pl. 7.

EXHIBITIONS: Washington, Phillips Collection, 1947, Drawings and Pastels by Edgar Degas, no. 31.
Philadelphia, Museum of Art, 1950-51, Masterpieces of Drawing, Diamond Jubilee Exhibition, no. 94, reprod.
Paris, 1955, no. 69, pl. 53.

EDGAR DEGAS

Paris 1834–Paris 1917

58 Young Woman in Street Costume

Brush drawing in transparent black wash and opaque black and white
body color on rose-beige paper. 12¾ x 9⅞ in. (325 x 250 mm.)
Signed below skirt at right in grey-blue chalk: degas   1965.260

The drawing, one of the best known and most beloved of Paul Sachs's
drawings, has figured in some exhibition almost every year since he acquired it. The number of such exhibitions in the United States and
abroad has passed the two dozen mark. The most important ones before 1955 are listed in the catalogue *French Drawings, Masterpieces
from Seven Centuries,* Chicago, Minneapolis, Detroit and San Francisco, 1955-56, no. 151, so we do not repeat them below.

PROVENANCE: Durand-Ruel to Paul J. Sachs.

BIBLIOGRAPHY: Mongan-Sachs, no. 669, fig. 345.
P. A. Lemoisne, *Degas,* Paris, 1946, II, no. 296.
Huyghe and Jacottet, *Le dessin français au XIXme siècle,*
Lausanne, 1948, pl. 95.
Klaus Berger, *Französische Meisterzeichnungen des neunzehn-
ten Jahrhunderts,* Basle, 1949, no. 41.
Shoolman and Slatkin, 1950, pl. 101.

EXHIBITIONS: See comment above. Also:
New York, Wildenstein, 1960, Degas, no. 81.
Baltimore, Museum of Art, 1962, Manet, Degas, Berthe Morisot
and Mary Cassatt, no. 36, reprod.

EDGAR DEGAS

Paris 1834–Paris 1917

59 A Ballet Dancer in Position Facing Three-Quarters Front

Soft graphite pencil accented with black crayon and heightened with white chalk on pink paper, squared for transfer. 16⅛ x 11¼ in. (410 x 284 mm.)
Signed at the lower right in pencil: degas   1965.263

The drawing is a study for the central figure in *La classe de danse,* Camondo Collection, Louvre (Lemoisne, no. 341), a figure which appears also in the background of three versions of the *Repétition d'un ballet sur la scène,* one in the Louvre and two in the Havemeyer Collection, Metropolitan Museum (Lemoisne nos. 340, 400 and 498). Another drawing in the Rotterdam Museum, sometimes identified as the same model, is inscribed by Degas *Josephine Gaujelin autrefois danseuse à l'Opera.* She is the dancer whose painted portrait by Degas is in the Isabella Stewart Gardner Museum, Boston. The Sachs drawing is not stamped with the atelier red stamp but is signed by the artist, probably at the same time that he signed the Joyant facsimile. Lillian Browse gives an exact technical ballet title *Danseuse en Quatrième Dernière, Pointe Tendue.* She does not accept the identification of the dancer as Josephine Gaujelin. The same dancer is seen in the same position, but from a different angle, in the Camondo, *Classe de Danse de M. Merante* (Lemoisne, no. 298) and the Metropolitan Museum's *Leçon de danse* (Lemoisne, no. 297).

PROVENANCE: First Degas Sale, Georges Petit Gallery, Paris, May 6-8, 1918, no. 328; César M. de Hauke to Paul J. Sachs, April 6, 1929.

BIBLIOGRAPHY: Mongan-Sachs, no. 670, fig. 346.
Rosenberg, 1959, p. 109.
Lillian Browse, *Edgar Degas Ballet Dancers,* London, 1960, no. 4.

EXHIBITIONS: San Francisco, 1940, no. 19, reprod. p. 85.
Rotterdam, Paris, New York, 1958-59, no. 166.

Degas

EDGAR DEGAS
Paris 1834–Paris 1917

60 Study for Portrait of Diego Martelli

Fabricated black chalk and white chalk on grey-brown paper. 17¾ x
11¼ in. (450 x 286 mm.)
The red stamp of the Degas Sale at the lower left (Lugt 658)   1965.255

The painting is now in the Museo de Bellas Artes, Buenos Aires. Another
Sachs drawing shows the full-length figure and is a study for the painting
now in the National Gallery of Scotland. A third drawing is in the
Cleveland Museum; a fourth, which belonged to Mlle. Fèvre, is now in
the collection of Sir Kenneth Clark. The last is inscribed in Degas' own
hand "Chez Martelli 3 avril 79." The Buenos Aires and Edinburgh portraits were shown in the Salon of 1879, so drawings and paintings were
done in the same year. Jean S. Boggs and Lamberto Vitali (see below)
have cleared up the confusion about the sitter's identity. Diego Martelli
(1833-96), a Florentine, interested in both the arts and letters, was a prom-
inent member of the group that used to meet in the Caffè Michelangiolo
and a friend of the painters known as the Macchiaioli. Degas probably
knew him first in Florence and later in Paris, where Martelli also knew
Corot, Millet, Daumier and Manet.

PROVENANCE: Third Degas Sale, Georges Petit Gallery, Paris, April 7-9, 1919,
no. 344A; César M. de Hauke to Paul J. Sachs, September, 1934.

BIBLIOGRAPHY: Mongan-Sachs, no. 673, fig. 349.
Watrous, 1957, pp. 114, 115.
Henry S. Francis, "Drawings by Degas," *Bulletin of the Cleve-
land Museum of Art,* XLIV, December, 1957, pp. 212-217.
Rosenberg, 1959, p. xxiii, also p. 110.
Peter A. Wick, "Degas Violinist," *Bulletin of the Museum of
Fine Arts,* Boston, 1959, LVII, no. 310, pp. 87-101.
Jean S. Boggs, *Portraits by Degas,* Berkeley, 1962, p. 123.
Lamberto Vitali, "Italian Friends of Degas," *Burlington Maga-
zine,* CV, 1963, pp. 266-273.

EXHIBITIONS: San Francisco, 1940, no. 21, reprod. p. 84.
Cleveland, Art Museum, 1947, Works by Edgar Degas, no. 68.
Paris, 1955, no. 71.

EDGAR DEGAS

Paris 1834–Paris 1917

61 After the Bath

Charcoal with additions of fabricated colored chalks on white paper.
17⅛ x 13⅛ in. (435 x 332 mm.)
Signed at the lower left: Degas   1965.259

This drawing is one of several bearing the same title in which the same
model, seen from behind, faces either to the left or to the right. The
group can be dated ca. 1885. A pastel of the same figure in the same pose
is in the William Rockill Nelson Gallery of Art in Kansas City.

PROVENANCE: Durand-Ruel to Paul J. Sachs.

BIBLIOGRAPHY: Mongan-Sachs, no. 674, fig. 350.
                Hilaire-Germain-Edgar Degas: Thirty Drawings and Pastels,
                   New York, 1944, pl. 11.
                Watrous, 1957, p. 116, reprod. p. 117.
                Rosenberg, 1959, p. xxiii, p. 116, reprod. no. 221.
                Jaromír Pečírka, *Drawings, Edgar Degas,* London, 1963, pl. 59.

EXHIBITIONS: Detroit, 1951, no. 37.

ADOLPH MENZEL   Breslau 1815–Berlin 1905

62   An Elderly Man in a Military Topcoat

Soft graphite pencil on white paper. 7⅞ x 4⅞ in. (200 x 125 mm.)
Signed and dated in pencil at the lower right: A.M.81.   1965.347

Two recent exhibitions of Menzel's drawings, a large and important one
held in Berlin in 1955, and another in Bremen in 1963, have again brought
the prolific nineteenth-century German draughtsman to public attention.
In 1832, at the age of sixteen, Menzel became the chief support of his widowed mother, brother and sister, when he took over his father's lithog-
raphy business. The habits of industry and accuracy, which he then developed, stood him in good stead throughout his long and productive life.
Famous in his lifetime as an historical painter, he is more widely known
today as a draughtsman of wide-ranging interests with a touch that is
both bold and controlled. Many surviving sketches are highly detailed
pencil studies, which show him examining and recording textures and
the play of light and shadow with the same steady eye that he turned on
himself in his self-portraits. This drawing, almost exactly the same size
as many pages from the sketchbooks of the sixties through the eighties,
may be an informal sketch of Bismarck, whose portrait Menzel had
painted ten years earlier. The artist favored this particular pose. Many
men and women are represented looking inward and downward. Menzel's left-handedness is not always as apparent as it is in the shading of
this solid figure.

PROVENANCE: Bollag to Paul J. Sachs.

BIBLIOGRAPHY: Mongan-Sachs, no. 434, fig. 214.

EXHIBITIONS: Minneapolis, 1962, University of Minnesota, and New York,
Guggenheim Museum, The Nineteenth Century: One Hun-
dred Twenty-five Master Drawings, no. 78.

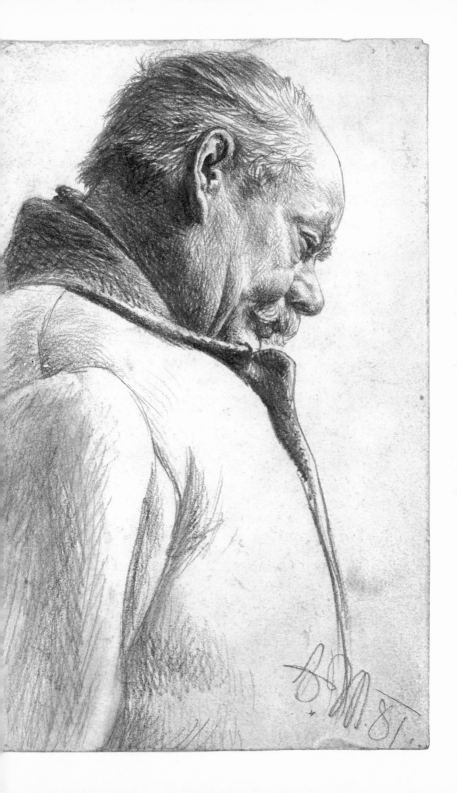

ODILON REDON   Bordeaux 1840–Paris 1916

63   Don Quixote

Black wax crayon, black chalk, pen and black ink and black wash on tracing paper, appliquéd to ivory drawing board. 11¼ x 8⅓⅓ in. (285 x 222 mm.); drawing board, 12⅝ x 9¾ in. (320 x 248 mm.)   1965.328

"Black is the most essential color," wrote Redon. "It conveys the very vitality of a being, his energy, his mind, something of his soul, the reflection of his sensitivity." This comment, cited by Mr. Sachs in his *Modern Prints and Drawings* (p. 55), suggests the spirit in which his *Don Quixote* can be appreciated. There is no single black. Instead Redon has built up an infinitely varied surface, playing off the accents of a pen line or delicate scraping against the dense shadows of black chalk and crayon. The result is a curiously iridescent form, appropriate to the haunting image of the knight and the tree. The subject is not documented; there is no reason, however, to doubt its traditional title, *Don Quixote*. Although undated, a stylistic comparison with Redon's lithographs suggests a date of ca. 1886. Sven Sandstrom, the author of *Le monde imaginaire d'Odilon Redon,* Lund, Sweden, 1955, suggested a date between 1885-90 with a reworking before 1895 (letter, May 15, 1955).

PROVENANCE: Weyhe to Paul J. Sachs, 1945.

BIBLIOGRAPHY: Sachs, 1954, pl. 49.
Jean Seznec, "Don Quixote and His French Illustrators," *Gazette des Beaux-Arts,* XXXIV, September, 1948, p. 187.
Bulletin of the Fogg Art Museum, XI, no. 1, January, 1949, p. 39.

PAUL GAUGUIN Paris 1848–Marquesas Islands 1903

64 Head of a Breton Peasant Girl

Graphite pencil, black and red crayon and black wash on white paper.
8¾ x 7⅞ in. (224 x 200 mm.)   1965.283

Concerning the quality of the drawing, there is no disagreement, but
there is a divergence of opinion concerning its date. Leymarie, who considers it one of the most beautiful of Gauguin's drawings in its monumental simplicity and human radiance, dates it from Gauguin's last
visit to Brittany in 1894, finding in its fullness of form and ease of style
an echo of Gauguin's South Seas' experience. With this opinion E. Mongan agrees. John Rewald and Richard Field note the strong similarities
to the figures in *Seaweed Gatherers,* Folkwang Museum, Essen, and the
Breton Girls (Private Collection, Paris) and date it about 1889.

PROVENANCE: Charles Vignier to Paul J. Sachs, 1923.

BIBLIOGRAPHY: Mongan-Sachs, no. 690, fig. 362.
John Rewald, *Gauguin Drawings,* New York, 1958, no. 14.
Jean Leymarie, *Paul Gauguin, Aquarelles, pastels, et dessins en
couleur,* Basel (Edition Phoebus), 1960, p. 27, reprod. Trans-
lated into English and published London (Faber), 1961, p.
27, reprod.
Moskowitz, III, no. 828.
René Huyghe, *Gauguin,* Milan, 1962, p. 27.

EXHIBITIONS: New York, Wildenstein, 1946, Paul Gauguin, no. 51.
Detroit, 1951, no. 42, reprod.
New York, Wildenstein, 1956, Gauguin, no. 67.
Chicago, Art Institute, and New York, Metropolitan Museum,
1959, Gauguin, no. 111.
Paris, Galerie Charpentier, 1960, Cent oeuvres de Gauguin, no.
56.
Munich, Haus der Kunst, 1960, Paul Gauguin, no. 86.
Vienna, Oberen Belvedere, 1960, Paul Gauguin, no. 25.

PABLO PICASSO

Malaga 1881–

65 Portrait of Fonte

Charcoal with blue, black and yellow wash on cream-colored paper.
20½ x 12⅛ in. (521 x 327 mm.)
Watermark: Shield surmounted by a crown
Signed across the lower part of the figure in charcoal: P. Ruiz Picasso

1965.321

The drawing reveals clearly the influence of Steinlen, but it may be that Steinlen's influence reached Picasso through Ramón Casas. Casas, whom Picasso knew at the influential Barcelona café, Quatre Gats, encouraged Picasso and passed on to him the influence of the French draughtsmen (A. H. Barr, *Picasso,* p. 16). Casas was a prolific artist whose portrait drawings, which show the influence of both Steinlen and Lautrec, are reproduced in great number in the periodical *Pèl y Ploma,* which he edited from 1899-1903. It was in 1901 that Picasso discarded the Spanish custom of the double patronymic, so the drawing must predate that year. The model, who wears a long artist's smock and holds an open book almost as though it were a painter's palette, was in fact a writer and, like Picasso, a Paris resident.

PROVENANCE: Perls Gallery to Paul J. Sachs, 1938.

BIBLIOGRAPHY: Mongan-Sachs, no. 739, fig. 398.
Alfred H. Barr, *Picasso, Fifty Years of His Art,* 1946, p. 280.

Forte   Forte

PABLO PICASSO

Malaga 1881–

66 A Mother Holding a Child and Four Studies of Her Right Hand

Verso: Standing Male Nude
Black crayon on cream-colored paper. 13½ x 10½ in. (342 x 266 mm.)
Signed in graphite pencil and dated at lower right: Picasso/1904

1965.318

The drawing is a study for the painting in the Göteborg Art Museum, Sweden. There is a pastel repeating the motif of mother and child, dated 1905, in an anonymous Swiss private collection. In the pastel the mother is nursing the child whose right hand is on her breast. She looks down tenderly in three-quarters view as here, not in profile as in the painting. John Richardson (visit 1958) was the first to suggest that the nude on the verso is a self-portrait. He noted its similarity to the *Self-Portrait* of 1901, still owned by the artist (Barr, p. 23). The drawing is at present and has been for some time the most popular drawing in the Fogg's collection.

PROVENANCE: Charles Vignier to Paul J. Sachs, Paris, December 10, 1929.

BIBLIOGRAPHY: Mongan-Sachs, no. 741, fig. 399.
M. Jardot, *Pablo Picasso Drawings,* 1959, no. 8, reprod.
Die Freuden des Lebens, Munich, 1960, p. 54, reprod.
Dessins de Pablo Picasso (Epoques bleue et rose), Mermod, 1960, no. 13, reprod.
Moskowitz, III, 1962, pl. 855.
Rosenberg, 1959, p. xxiv, p. 125, reprod. no. 228.
Anthony Blunt and Phoebe Pool, *Picasso, the Formative Years,* New York, 1962, pl. 133.

EXHIBITIONS: Rotterdam, Paris, New York, 1958-59, no. 211, pl. 211.
Toronto, Art Gallery and Montreal, Museum of Fine Arts, Picasso and Man, 1964, no. 20, reprod.

PABLO PICASSO

Malaga 1881 –

67 The Bathers

Graphite pencil on white paper. 9½ x 12¼ in. (230 x 310 mm.)
Signed and dated at the lower right: Picasso 18   1965.319

According to Alfred Barr the drawing was done at Biarritz (*Picasso-
Seventy-fifth Anniversary Exhibition*, Museum of Modern Art, 1957,
no. 80). Earlier he had written: "It is one of Picasso's most elaborate
figure compositions and combines fifteen figures with extraordinary
grace and subtlety. The distortions ... may have been inspired by Ingres,
but they appear in many periods ... there is nothing obviously deriva-
tive about such a drawing" (Picasso, *Fifty Years of His Art*, New York,
1946, p. 102).

PROVENANCE: Paul Rosenberg, Paris, to Paul J. Sachs, April, 1920.

BIBLIOGRAPHY: Mongan-Sachs, no. 742, fig. 400.
               Frank Seiberling, *Looking into Art*, New York, 1959, pp. 133
                  and 135, fig. 93.
               Maurice Jardot, *Pablo Picasso, Drawings*, New York, 1959, p.
                  48, reprod.

EXHIBITIONS: Rotterdam, Paris, New York, 1958-59, no. 218, pl. 220.
               New York, Duveen Gallery, 1962, Picasso-An American Tribute,
                  no. 1.
               Minneapolis, University of Minnesota; New York, Guggenheim
                  Museum; Cambridge, Fogg Art Museum; 1963-64, 20th Cen-
                  tury Master Drawings, no. 103.

DIEGO RIVERA   Guanajuato 1886–San Angel 1957

68   Madame Fisher

Graphite pencil on white paper. 18⅜ x 12⅛ in. (472 x 309 mm.)
Watermark: ARCHES
Inscribed by the artist at the lower left: Madame Fisher/Diego Rivera
VI-18   1965.437

Rivera arrived in Europe, on his second journey, in December, 1911.
During the next few years he was in Paris on and off, alternately ab-
sorbed in the Paris scene and in painting away from Paris, in Madrid,
Barcelona and Majorca. He was one of the few artists whose life and
work was not completely disrupted by the war, but the cataclysm posed
problems even for those not immediately involved. By 1918 Rivera's ex-
periments with Cubism and Futurism were behind him. It was the year
when Cézanne's influence was paramount, but it was also the year when
he was studying the work of the old masters, David, Holbein and, one
suspects here, even Ingres. For the time being his personal characteristics,
above all his "Mexicanism," were submerged. A group of drawings dated
1918, like this one, show great exactitude, finesse and delicacy and a sen-
timent that is reflective and withdrawn. It was a style which was not
sympathetic to him nor suitable for what he felt was his historic calling.
In 1919 he "determined deliberately to kill everything in his own work
which was not his own" (Jere Abbott, Museum of Modern Art catalogue, see below). He went off to Italy and there found the means of his
liberation. We have been unable to identify Madame Fisher.

PROVENANCE: E. Weyhe to Paul J. Sachs, 1929.

EXHIBITIONS: New York, Museum of Modern Art, 1931-32, Diego Rivera, no.
81.
Mexico City, Museo Nacional de Artes Plasticas, 1951, Diego
Rivera, 50 años de su labor artistica, no. 108.

Madame Fichte
f fingo Bruay VI 14

GEORGE BELLOWS

Columbus, Ohio 1882–New York 1925

69 Lady Jean

Lithographic crayon on white paper. 22 x 13½ in. (559 x 354 mm.)

1965.104

The drawing is a study for the painting *Lady Jean,* formerly in the Stephen Clark Collection and bequeathed by him to the Yale Art Gallery. The painting, one of Bellows' most beloved works, was painted at Woodstock, New York, in the summer of 1924, less than six months before the artist's death. The drawing must have preceded it by a very short time. All the members of the Bellows family liked to "dress up." One day that summer, Jean, the younger of the artist's two daughters, dressed up in a dress made about 1870 for a very small woman (Frances R. Nugent, *George Bellows,* New York, 1963, p. 33) given her by a southern lady "to wear to a party." Jean was then nine years old. Her father was so enchanted with her appearance that he painted her wearing the dress. A comparison of the figure in the drawing with that in the painting reveals only slight changes of detail.

PROVENANCE: Rehn Gallery to Paul J. Sachs, 1934.

EXHIBITIONS: Chicago, Art Institute, 1946, George Bellows, Paintings, Drawings and Prints, no. 76, reprod. p. 81.
Philadelphia, Museum of Art, 1950-51, Masterpieces of Drawing, no. 112, reprod.
Washington, National Gallery, 1957, George Bellows, no. 74, reprod. p. 107.
Rouen, Musée des Beaux-Arts, 1960, Dessins américains du XVIIIe siècle à nos jours, no. 6, reprod. on cover.

GEORGE GROSZ   Berlin 1893–Berlin 1959

70   Portrait of Anna Peter

Graphite pencil with stumping on white Ingres paper. 26⅝ x 21 in.
Signed at the lower right: Grosz
Gift of Paul J. Sachs to the Museum of Modern Art, 1929   4.29

In 1920 Grosz married Eva Louise Peter, and in 1926 their first son
Peter was born. It was during this period of the mid-twenties that the
acid satire of his earlier work was richly complemented by a series of
family portraits, including the 1925 *Portrait of the Artist's Mother* and
the studies of *Grandma Peter* done in 1926-27. Among the latter is this
monumental drawing. The vigorous rhythm of his pencil line, softened
by stumping, communicates an alertness and competence in his mother-
in-law. It also harmonizes Grosz' formal interests both in subtleties of
texture and massive form. This was the first drawing acquired by the
Museum of Modern Art, given by Mr. Sachs only a few days after the
museum had opened in October, 1929.

BIBLIOGRAPHY: G. Grosz, *George Grosz Drawings,* New York, 1944, pl. 10.
William S. Lieberman, "Drawings: Recent Acquisitions, An
Announcement of the Paul J. Sachs Committee," *Museum of
Modern Art Bulletin,* xxix, no. 1, 1962, p. 4.

EXHIBITIONS: New York, Museum of Modern Art, 1941, Paintings, Drawings,
Prints by George Grosz, circulating exhibition, p. 3.
New York, Museum of Modern Art, 1944, Modern Drawings, p.
91.

CHARLES SHEELER Philadelphia 1883–Irvington-on-Hudson 1965

71 Totems in Steel

Conté crayon on white paper. 19⅛ x 22¾ in. (485 x 577 mm.)
Signed at lower right: Sheeler 1935   1965.148

In a foreword to the exhibition of his work at the Museum of Modern Art in 1939, an exhibition in which this drawing was included, Charles Sheeler wrote, "From the casual portrayal of the momentary appearance of nature learned in art school, to the concept of a picture as having an underlying architectural structure to support the elements in nature which comprise the picture, was a long journey. ..." He went on to compare his interest in photography and in painting, finding that the two interests were parallel, not competitive, "the painting being the result of a composite image and the photograph being the result of a single image." His first trip to Italy in 1909 (his third journey abroad) was a milestone, for he discovered in Giotto and Piero della Francesca that "a picture could be assembled arbitrarily with a concern for design" (Constance Rourke, see below). This he had not learned in Chase's studio. His work a little later as a photographer of houses for Philadelphia architects must have strengthened his interest in structure, as did his 1927 photographs of the Ford Plant at River Rouge. The easily overlooked figure at the left, once seen, immediately gives another dimension to these striking mechanical forms and their penetration of space. Not all the interest of the drawing lies in its formal values. A small tempera (3¾ x 5 in.) with the same title was no. 99 of the Museum of Modern Art Exhibition (Mr. and Mrs. O'Donnell Iselin).

PROVENANCE: The Downtown Gallery to Paul J. Sachs.

BIBLIOGRAPHY: Constance Rourke, *Charles Sheeler, Artist in the American Tradition,* New York, 1938, p. 167.

EXHIBITIONS: New York, Museum of Modern Art, 1939, Charles Sheeler, Paintings, Drawings, Photographs, no. 100.
Brooklyn, Museum, 1957, American Drawings, 1905-56, p. 35.
Iowa City, University of Iowa, 1963, Retrospective Exhibition of the Art of Charles Sheeler, no. 43.

PAVEL TCHELICHEW

Moscow 1898–Grotto-
ferrata 1957

72 Portrait Studies of Nicolas Kopeikine

Silver point and graphite pencil on white prepared paper. 18⅞ x 12⅜ in.
(478 x 214 mm.)
Signed at the bottom center: P. Tchelichew '37   1959.166

According to James Soby (*Tchelichew,* Museum of Modern Art, New
York, 1942, pp. 28-29) the artist, while he was working on his important
painting *Phenomena* and a series of portraits, developed a deep interest
in the medium of silver point. This was in 1935 and the years immediately following. The portrait of Kopeikine, Kirstein records, was drawn
in the spring of 1937 in the artist's studio. Kopeikine was a Russian
pianist whom Tchelichew met in New York. The musician and the
painter shared an interest in ballet, and both were friends of Georges
Balanchine. Here are discernible the beginnings of Tchelichew's interest in the multiple image and in metamorphosis. The coat collar begins
to turn into a porcupine and there is a Janus-like head between the profile view and the full face. Kirstein records that in addition to the separate drawings of Kopeikine's hands which he reproduces (pl. 10), Tchelichew also made drawings of him dressed as a child prodigy and in
various operatic disguises. Other silver point portraits of him belong to
Dr. Burrill B. Crohn and Edaldji Dinsha, both of New York.

PROVENANCE: Durlacher Brothers to Paul J. Sachs, 1943.

BIBLIOGRAPHY: Lincoln Kirstein, *Tchelichew Drawings,* New York, 1947, p. 19,
no. 32.
Watrous, pp. 8-90.
Sachs, 1954, p. 229, pl. 202.

EXHIBITIONS: New York, Museum of Modern Art, 1944, p. 98, no. 85.

HENRI MATISSE   Le Cateau, Picardy 1869–Cimiez
1954

73   A Lady with a Necklace

Pen and black ink on white paper. 21¼ x 17¾ in. (540 x 450 mm.)
Signed and dated at the lower left: Henri Matisse 36   1965.307

The model for the drawing was Lydia Delectorskaya, the blue-eyed
blonde Russian who, beginning in 1935, can be recognized as the model
for many of Matisse's most successful paintings and drawings. R. Escholier (*Matisse,* New York, 1960, p. 155) wrote that "her plastic splendour,
beauty and expression of face, intelligence and wit" constantly inspired
the artist. Matisse made a series of drawings of her wearing a Balkan
blouse. According to Alfred H. Barr (*Matisse,* New York, 1951, p. 223)
she later became and remained the artist's "loyal secretary and buffer
against intrusion." Matisse, in explaining his own drawings, wrote in *le
Point* (July, 1939), "My line drawing is the purest and most direct trans-
lation of my emotion. Simplification of means allows that. But those
drawings are more complete than they appear to some people who con-
fuse them with a sketch. They generate light; looked at in a poor, or
indirect light, they contain not only quality and sensibility, but also
light and differences in values corresponding obviously to color ... the
drawings are always preceded by studies made in a less vigorous medium ... it is not until I feel exhausted by that work, which may go on
for several sessions, that I can with a clear mind give run to my pen
without hesitation" (quoted by Escholier, p. 123).

PROVENANCE: Paul Rosenberg to Paul J. Sachs, 1938.

BIBLIOGRAPHY: Mongan-Sachs, no. 735, fig. 394.
Gianni Testori, *Matisse, 25 Disegni,* Milan, 1943, pl. 10.
Watrous, 1957, p. 150.
Agnes Humbert, *Henri Matisse, Dessins,* Paris, 1956, pl. 10.

HENRY MOORE   Castleford (Yorkshire) 1898–

74   Study for the Northampton Madonna

Black and orange grease crayon, pen and black ink, and black wash over pencil on white paper. The highlights were first drawn with a light waxy substance that repelled subsequent layers of wash. 9 x 7 in. (228 x 177 mm.)

Inscribed at the upper right: Moore 42

Verso: Sketch in graphite pencil of a woman reclining in a landscape.

1958.24

On February 19, 1944, a statue of the Madonna and Child carved by Henry Moore in green Hornton stone was unveiled in St. Matthew's Church, Northampton, England. The imaginative vicar of St. Matthew's, Canon Hussey, had commissioned the work because he had been struck by Moore's drawings of mothers protecting their children in the London air-raid shelters. He had found the drawings extraordinarily moving in both spiritual and human terms. Moore had explored the theme of the mother and child throughout his career, sometimes with an almost Cycladic simplicity (*Mother and Child,* 1931, Kearnly Collection), at others, as here, with a new monumentality of scale and concern for expressive gesture. "The Madonna and Child should have an austerity and a nobility and some touch of grandeur (even hieratic aloofness)," wrote Moore, "which is missing in the everyday 'Mother and Child' idea" (J. J. Sweeney, *Henry Moore,* Museum of Modern Art, New York, 1946, p. 81). The bold rhythms and massiveness of the Sachs drawing reflect his search for these qualities. The free pencil sketch on the verso suggests some of Moore's large bronze reclining figures.

PROVENANCE: Curt Valentin to Paul J. Sachs, 1946.

BEN SHAHN

Koons, Lithuania 1898–

75 Man Picking Wheat *or* Beatitudes

Pen and black ink on white paper. 38 x 25 in. (960 x 635 mm.)
Signed in ink in lower right: Ben Shahn   1955.162

The second title is that written below the wood engraving, with some
color, which Shahn designed and Baskin engraved. Paul Sachs gave the
print to the museum when he presented the drawing. Soby (see below)
dates the drawing 1950. There is also a serigraph which differs slightly
from the drawing. For the woodcut, the figure of the man and a large
drawing of a wheat field (reproduced as end papers of Soby's book) were
made into a single composition. Selden Rodman in his monograph on
Ben Shahn (New York, 1951) introduces his subject thus: "To understand the imagery of an artist whose work extracts universal meanings
from a real world, it is helpful to know everything that can be known
about that artist. ..." When queried about the *Man Picking Wheat*
(conversation, August 17, 1965), Ben Shahn said that when he, a city-
bred person, went to live in Roosevelt, New Jersey, he looked at the
countryside with new eyes. He added that he meant the gesture of the
man picking the wheat to have a hieratic significance. Further conversation revealed long thoughts and memories. He spoke of his childhood
in Russia and of his grandparents waiting for the harvest, and of a memory of his grandfather walking through a field of tall ripening grain,
estimating the quality of the crop and the meaning of that estimate.

PROVENANCE: Downtown Gallery to Paul J. Sachs, 1955.

BIBLIOGRAPHY: Ben Shahn, *Paragraphs on Art*, Roosevelt, N. J., 1952, reprod. p.
                7.
                Sachs, 1954, p. 235, pl. 209.
                James Thrall Soby, *Ben Shahn*, New York, 1957, p. 19, pl. 50.

EXHIBITIONS: Venice, Biennale XXVII, 1954, no. 61.
               Cambridge, Fogg Art Museum, 1957, The Art of Ben Shahn,
               no. 67.

CHINESE   Late Shang or Western Chou (ca. 11th-9th Century B.C.)

76 Pendant in the shape of an animal head

Lapis lazuli   h. 1⅝ in.   1965.465

Although lapis lazuli is rarely seen among early Chinese stone carvings, the type and design of this object point to its Chinese provenance and a date about Late Shang or Western Chou.

CHINESE Late Chou or Early Han (ca. 3rd-1st Century B.C.)

77 Weight composed of three griffins (winged felines) surrounding a cone and carrying a small mountain peak

Bronze   h. 2¼ in.; diam. 2¾ in.   1965.466

JAPANESE   Fujiwara Period (897-1185 A.D.)

78 Votive plaque representing the Buddhist deity Muijū
Rikikū, one of the Godai Rikikū

Bronze   h. 15½ in.; w. 9 in.

Gift of Meta and Paul J. Sachs in memory of Langdon Warner   1955.139

CAMBODIAN   10th-11th Century A.D.

79 Buddhist Divinity

Stone   h. 16 in.   1943.1

Although Paul Sachs gave this sculpture to the Fogg in 1943, he first lent it to
the museum as early as 1926, so it has long been identified with his collection.
There seems to be no record of where or precisely when he acquired it.

CAMBODIAN   Khmer Period, 13th Century A.D.

80 Head of a Buddha

Stone   h. 8½ in.   1928.165

PROVENANCE: Paul Mallon to Kelekian to Paul J. Sachs, 1918-19.

When, in 1922, Paul Sachs lent this head to the Fogg Museum, the learned
Dr. Denman W. Ross published it (*Fogg Museum Notes,* June, 1922). Dr.
Ross, a great connoisseur, was one of the few Americans who had then been
in Angkor Vat and who had studied the little known Cambodian civilization.
He described the head as one of the finest he had seen anywhere, either in
Cambodia or in Paris, where French savants were then beginning to collect
and study the work of Khmer sculptors.

CHINESE   Late Tang Dynasty (9th Century?)

81 Seated Figure of the Bodhisattva Mañjuśrī (Chinese,
    Wen-shu)

Gilt bronze   h. 4$\frac{9}{16}$ in.   1965.467

The figure is seated like an ascetic, with a small book in his left hand. The
attribute held in his right hand is lost.

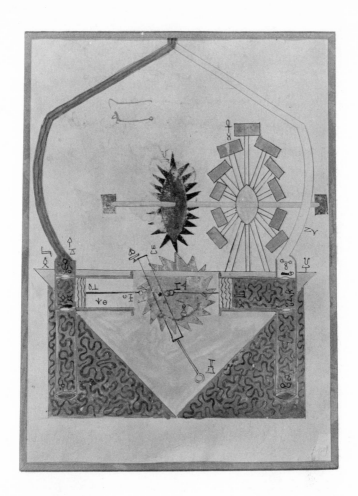

MUHAMMAD IBN AHMAD

Attributed to Arab, 14th Century

82 Illustration of a mechanical device for raising water in a flowing stream, described in the fifth section of the fifth chapter of this fourteenth-century copy of al-Jazari's treatise on Automata (1206). Cairo (?), 1354

Gouache on coarse yellowish paper $15\frac{3}{16}$ x $10\frac{15}{16}$ in.

Verso: Text written by "the Smyrnan," Muhammad ibn Ahmad al-Izmiri

PROVENANCE: F. R. Martin (who obtained it in Constantinople); Paul J. Sachs.

BIBLIOGRAPHY: Ananda K. Coomaraswamy, *The Treatise of al-Jazari on Auto-mata,* Boston, Museum of Fine Arts (Communications to the Trustees, VI), 1924, pp. 17, 18, pl. VII.

GREEK Attic School (?) 4th Century B.C.

83 Head of an Athlete

Parian marble h. 12¼ in. 1922.171

PROVENANCE: A. Kann, Paris, to Paul J. Sachs, 1920.

The Head's exact date has been debated by classical archaeologists and remains an open question. It has been published as a provincial work of the fourth century, but the possibility that it is an excellent Roman copy has been raised in recent years.

FRENCH ROMANESQUE   12th Century

84 Capital: Scenes from the Story of Samson

Carrara marble   h. 12½ in.; w. at top, 10½ in.; w. at base, 7 in.

1922.132

PROVENANCE: From the Cloister of Notre-Dame-des-Doms, the Cathedral of
               Avignon; Garcin Collection; d'Hendecourt, Paris, to Paul J.
               Sachs, 1920.

The capital illustrates four events from the story of Samson: Samson wres-
tling with the lion (illustrated above); Samson carrying off the Gates of
Gaza; Delilah cutting off Samson's hair; and Samson and the Philistines.

MASTER OF THE FOGG PIETÀ Florence, Second Quarter of the 14th Century

85 Mourning over the Body of Christ

Tempera on panel   16 x 19 in. (sight)

PROVENANCE: Marchese della Robbia, Florence; Tedeschi, Rome; Durlacher, London, to Paul J. Sachs, 1920.

Gift of Paul J. Sachs, in memory of Grace Norton   1927.306

The painting was attributed by the late Richard Offner who grouped around it a number of other panels which are clearly by the same hand, although the given name of the artist remains unknown. Grace Norton, one of Charles Eliot Norton's daughters, had been brought up in the house at Shady Hill. In her last years she became a great friend of Paul Sachs.

AMBROGIO LORENZETTI

Sienese, active 1319-1348

86 The Crucifixion, ca. 1337-42

Tempera on panel

24 x 11¾ in.

PROVENANCE: Cyril B. Harcourt, London (as Cavallini); C. Fairfax Murray, London; John E. Murray, Florence, to Paul J. Sachs, 1919.

Gift of Paul J. Sachs, in honor of Edward W. Forbes's thirtieth year as Director of the Fogg Museum.

1939.113

The painting was exhibited at the Royal Academy, London, in 1879. It then bore an attribution to Cavallini. In 1916, Mr. Forbes and Mr. Sachs began negotiating for its purchase for the Fogg Museum through C. Fairfax Murray's son, John, who was then in Florence. Italy was about to declare war and the negotiations were somewhat agitated. In order to assure its purchase Mr. Sachs bought it himself. Twenty years later he presented it to the Fogg Museum in honor of Edward W. Forbes.

OSSERVANZA MASTER   Sienese, Second Quarter of the 15th
Century

87 Christ in Limbo

Tempera on panel   13½ x 17 in.

PROVENANCE: Earl of Northesk (purchased in Rome, ca. 1860, by W. Hope-
town, Eighth Earl of Northesk); R. Langton Douglas, London,
to Paul J. Sachs, 1915.

Gift of Paul J. Sachs, Class of 1900, "A testimonial to my friend Edward W.
Forbes"   1922.172

For many years the panel was attributed to Sassetta but, in 1956, Professor
Millard Meiss suggested that it was more probably by the Osservanza Master,
an unnamed painter in Sassetta's circle.

JUAN DE BURGOS

Spanish, ca. 1450

88 Annunciation

Tempera on panel

Diptych

Gabriel panel: 36 x 13$\frac{15}{16}$ in.

Virgin panel: 36$\frac{1}{4}$ x 13$\frac{15}{16}$ in.

PROVENANCE: Discovered in Madrid, ca. 1870, by J. C. Robinson, London; Klein-
berger Galleries, New York, to Paul J. Sachs, 1916.

Signed at the lower right beneath the figure of the angel on a "cartellino":
Maestre/Jū de Bur/gos pitor   1928.168

Sir Charles Robinson, who discovered these paintings in Madrid about 1870,
was director of the South Kensington Museum and, from 1882 until the death
of Victoria, "Surveyor of the Queen's Pictures." He traveled widely on the
continent, purchasing paintings and drawings, many of which he later sold.
Lugt describes him as "one of the most sagacious and erudite connoisseurs of
his epoch." No other certain work by Juan de Burgos is known. Each panel
is in its original elaborate gold frame.

MASTER OF ST. GUDULE

Flemish, Fourth Quarter of
the 15th Century

89 Christ in the Garden of Gethsemane

Oil on panel

49½ x 22¾ in.

PROVENANCE: Ehrich Galleries, New York, to Paul J. Sachs.

A panel in the Louvre, the *Sermon of a Saint,* is the key picture around which
scholars have reconstructed the *oeuvre* of an anonymous Flemish painter
active during the last quarter of the fifteenth century. His name refers to the
towers of St. Gudule, the Cathedral of Brussels, which rise in the background
of the painting. The attribution of our panel to the Master of St. Gudule was
originally suggested by Friedrich Winkler. First loaned to the Fogg Art Museum in 1926, the painting was given to Harvard in 1950 and subsequently
transferred to the Busch-Reisinger Museum. (For other works by the Master
of St. Gudule, see Max J. Friedländer, *Die Altniederländische Malerei,* IV
Hugo van der Goes, Berlin, 1926, p. 112ff., pls. 70-78.)

JACOPO ROBUSTI, called TINTORETTO

Venetian, 1518-1594

90 Allegory of Fidelity, ca. 1578

Oil on canvas (unfinished)   43¼ x 41 in.

PROVENANCE: Friedrich Nerly to John Ruskin, 1852; to Arthur Severn; Ehrich
Galleries, New York, to Samuel Sachs, 1915.

Gift of Mrs. Samuel Sachs, in memory of Mr. Samuel Sachs   1942.165

In a letter to his father from Venice, February 13, 1852, Ruskin described the
painting. "Of course it is very slight and a mere sketch, or it would fetch more
money (Ruskin was hoping his father would reimburse him for his expendi-
ture), but a grand thing—about a quarter of an hour of the man's handling
altogether, but the suggestion of a complete picture." (*Stones of Venice,* III, in
The Works of Ruskin, ed. E. T. Cook and A. Wedderburn, London, 1904, XI,
p. 376.) When Ruskin acquired it, it was attributed to Veronese, an attribution he quickly changed. Paul Sachs recommended the painting to *his* father.
It was then thought to represent Diana, but the late Dr. Suida identified it as
one of a series of allegories of the Virtues. This one would be an Allegory of
Fidelity.

NICOLAS POUSSIN
French, 1594-1665

91 The Holy Family, ca. 1650-51

Oil on canvas

38½ x 51 in. 1942.168

PROVENANCE: Painted for le duc de Créquy. When it belonged later to Froment de Veine it was engraved by Pesne. Collection Hariague Sale, Paris, April 14, 1750, no. 10; Peilhon, Paris, May 16, 1763; duc des Deux Ponts, Paris, April 6, 1778, no. 59; Robit, Paris, May 11, 1801, no. 88; Hibbert; Lord Radstock (1824); Christie Sale, May 13, 1826; Sir Simon Clarke Sale, May 8, 1840, no. 49; Thomas Hope Sale, Christie's, July 20, 1917, no. 68, to Tooth; Richard Owen to Samuel Sachs, 1923.

The painting is among the most beautiful of several classical *Holy Families* by Poussin. It was painted when landscape was becoming of increasing importance to the artist. The bath which the Madonna prepares for the Child is a symbol of purification and redemption. Paul Sachs urged his father, with success, to purchase the painting when it arrived in New York. It was presented to the Fogg Museum by Mrs. Samuel Sachs in memory of her husband, Samuel Sachs.

NICOLAS POUSSIN
French, 1594-1665

92 The Infant Bacchus Entrusted to The Nymphs, 1657

Oil on canvas $48\frac{5}{16}$ x $70\frac{1}{2}$ in.

PROVENANCE: Commissioned by Jacques Stella, 1657; Marquis de Montcalm, Montpellier; duc d'Orléans, 1795; Willett Willet, 1819; Chevalier Erard, Paris, 1833; Adrian Hope Sale, Christie's, June 30, 1894, no. 55; Sir A. Hayter; Durlacher Bros., London, to Samuel Sachs, 1923.

Gift of Mrs. Samuel Sachs in memory of Mr. Samuel Sachs   1942.167

Stella, who commissioned the picture, was a painter and art dealer in Rome. The painting is an elaborate allegory at several levels of meaning. Mercury brings the newborn Bacchus down from Jupiter to be raised by the nymphs who recline near a grotto which is entwined with vine leaves and filled with jars of wine. The god Pan plays on his pipes in a grove above. At the right Narcissus dies of self-love and the spurned Echo turns slowly to stone. Life is contrasted with death, fertility with sterility and the divine with the human. Paul Sachs bought the painting for his father in London in 1923.

ALBRECHT DÜRER German, 1471-1528

93   The Four Riders of the Apocalypse

Woodcut, before text 15½ x 11⅛ in.
B. 64, K.109

PROVENANCE: H. S. Theobald; Paul J. Sachs to Fogg Art Museum, 1943.

This brilliant impression of the *Four Riders* was always one of Mr. Sachs'
favorite prints. For many years it hung in the hall at Shady Hill. He used
the print often in teaching as an outstanding example of what a fine Dürer
woodcut could and should be.

REMBRANDT VAN RIJN   Dutch, 1606-1667

94   The Great Jewish Bride, 1635

Etching   8⅝ x 6⅝ in.

B.340; H.127   M208

PROVENANCE: British Museum Duplicate; Paul J. Sachs to Fogg Art Museum, 1911.

This was the first print given by Mr. Sachs to the Fogg Art Museum, on March 6, 1911. He was doubtless very pleased to be able to present to the Fogg a famous Rembrandt subject which had the cachet of the British Museum.

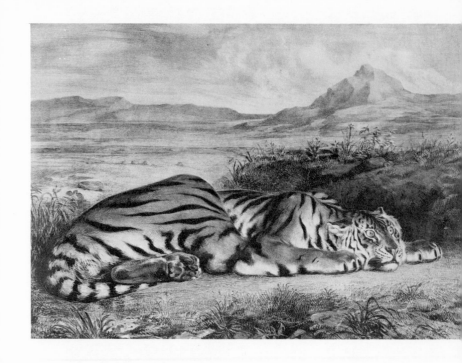

EUGÈNE DELACROIX

French, 1798-1863

95 Royal Tiger, 1829

Lithograph, third state $12\frac{9}{16}$ x $18\frac{1}{4}$ in.

Del. 80   M2,154

PROVENANCE: Dr. A. M. Klipstein; Keppel to Paul J. Sachs, 1922; to the Fogg Art Museum, May 23, 1922.

The collector, in his choice of this print, was not so much interested in the representation of a wild beast *per se,* as he was in owning a magistral lithograph by the great Romantic artist who, in an idiom new to the nineteenth century, evoked some of the color and energy of Rubens and the great Venetians.

EDGAR DEGAS
French, 1834-1917

96 Portrait of the Engraver Joseph Tourny

Etching, second state
D.4

8⅞ x 5⅝ in.
M14,295 (1965)

The collector's choice of this sensitive portrait speaks for itself. In one masterly etching there is encompassed Paul Sachs' long predilection for both Rembrandt and Degas. The youthful Degas etched with finesse and perception the figure of his friend and mentor, the engraver and water-colorist Joseph Tourny (1817-1880). For his composition he borrowed from Rembrandt's *Self-Portrait at a Window*. The print was made in Rome in the winter of 1856-1857.

EDGAR DEGAS

French, 1834-1917

97 La Famille Cardinal, 1880

Monotype

8½ x 6⁵⁄₁₆ in.   M14,295 (1965)

The monotypes of Degas have a distinct, subtle quality. For a long time they were ignored by print collectors because they did not fit into the traditional categories of graphic techniques. Because of his astute understanding of the artist, Paul Sachs recognized, long before most other collectors, their unique quality. This scene was planned as one of the illustrations for a book, *La Famille Cardinal,* by Degas' friend Ludovic Halévy. It was Degas' only attempt to make book illustrations and the project was abandoned before completion. The illustrations which Degas prepared have, however, been reproduced in a modern edition (Paris, Auguste Blaizot et Fils, 1939).

HENRI DE TOULOUSE-LAUTREC   French, 1864-1901

98 Miss Ida Heath, 1896

Lithograph   14¼ x 10⅜ in.
Del. 165   M13,201 (1956)

The fact that Lautrec admired, indeed, reverenced the work of Degas, early
inclined Paul Sachs to look with favor upon the younger artist's own work,
long before Lautrec's name or *oeuvre* was familiar in America. Although he
admired the paintings, Mr. Sachs had a particular love of Lautrec's deft and
deliberate irony in black and white.

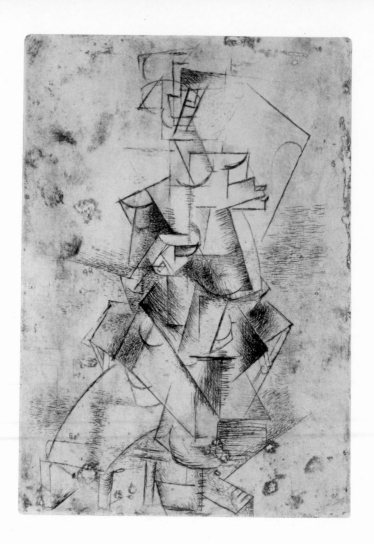

PABLO PICASSO   Spanish, 1881-

99 Mlle. Léonie in a Chaise Longue, 1910 (Saint Martorel,
    Plate III)

Etching and dry point, unique second state   7¾ x 5⅝ in.
G.25   M12,908 (1954)

Picasso's illustrations for the little paperback books of his friend Max Jacob,
the cubist, are perhaps the most fugitive sheets in the artist's entire work.
They are to be read not as commentary, but as complementing the elusive
text.

PABLO PICASSO

Spanish, 1881-

100 Satyr and Sleeping Woman, 1936

Aquatint   12½ x 16½ in.
Vollard Suite, 27   M13,164 (1956)

It is characteristic that when, late in his collecting activity, Mr. Sachs came to select a Picasso print, he instinctively chose the most important plate in the Vollard Suite. Doubtless the overtones of Tiepolo and Goya, which are reflected in this aquatint, made it singularly attractive to him.

Index

Supplement

Check List of the Paul J. Sachs Collection

NOTE: An asterisk indicates that the object is included in the exhibition and is therefore illustrated in the catalogue.

Watercolors have been classified as drawings rather than as paintings.

Under each classification the objects have, with a single exception, Islamic Art, been listed alphabetically.

Generous gifts of textiles and furniture have not been listed.

A summary, according to media and national schools, indicates the variety of prints given.

The numbers following each title are the Fogg Museum accession numbers and will be the photographer's numbers.

This check list has been compiled in order to suggest the range of Paul Sachs's interests and the magnitude of his generosity.

The total of objects listed to date is over 2,690.

Antiquities

Egyptian, *Arm of a Statue,* wood, 1965.469.
Egyptian, *Statuette of a Man,* wood, 1965.470.
Egyptian, *Torso,* wood, 1929.265.
*Greek, Attic School(?), *Head of an Athlete,* marble, 1922.171.
Greek, *Small Two-handled Vase,* 1965.488.
Roman Copy of Greek, *Head of Ares,* Pentelic marble, 1956.9.
Roman, first century B.C., *Detail of Façade,* marble, 1926.31.2.
Roman, *Small Statuette of a Goddess,* silver, 1942.233.
Roman, Early Republican, *Denarius,* silver, 1942.229.
Scythian, *Plaque Representing a Tiger,* bronze, 1927.13.

Islamic Art

Miniatures and Calligraphies

Arab, A.D. 1224, School of Baghdad, Folio from a manuscript of the *Materia Medica* by Dioscorides, *Birds and Flowers,* 1965.478.

*Arab, A.D. 1354, School of Cairo(?), Folio from a manuscript of al-Jazarī's treatise on Automata (1206), *A Device for Raising Water,* 1965.476.

Ten Folios of Calligraphy, Arabic and Persian, eighth-eighteenth centuries: 1920.21, 1927.160, 1927.162-164, 1927.166-169, 1965.484.

Timurid, Provincial Style, ca. 1450, *Rustam Rescues Bizhan from a Pit,* Folio from a manuscript of the *Shahnama,* 1965.480.

Turkoman Style, ca. 1490, *Battle Scene,* from a manuscript of the *Khamsa* of Nizami, 1965.481.

Bukhara Style, ca. 1560, *Timur Hunting,* from a manuscript of the *Zafarnama,* 1965.477.

Safavid, School of Shiraz, ca. 1560-70, *Rustam and Rakhsh Slay a Dragon,* from a manuscript of the *Shahnama,* 1965.479.

Safavid, School of Shiraz, ca. 1580, *A Prince Enthroned, with Courtiers and Attendants,* 1965.482.

Safavid, School of Isfahan, ca. 1600, *Lady Holding a Cup and Carafe,* 1965.483.

Persian Ceramics

Early Islamic Period, *Bowl,* porcelain, 1965.491.

Eleventh century, Rhages, *Shallow Bowl,* four-legged animal in center, 1965.489.

Twelfth century, Rhages, *Hexagonal Bowl,* 1965.490.

Twelfth century, *Gray Deep Bowl,* porcelain, 1949.24.

Thirteenth century, *Bowl from Sultanabad,* porcelain, 1965.492.

Oriental Painting and Sculpture

Chinese Sculpture

Chinese, *Belt Buckle,* bronze, 1949.29.

Chinese(?), *Head of a Serpent Mounted on a Wooden Base,* gilt bronze, 1965.493.

Ch'ing Dynasty, *Bottle-shaped Vase,* 1965.487.

*Late Chou or Early Han Dynasty, *Coffin Weight,* bronze, 1965.466.

Ming Dynasty, *Ovoid Jar,* 1965.486.

Ming Dynasty, *Box Lid,* stone, 1927.15.

Ordos(?), *Pierced Plaque with Goat,* bronze, 1943.1843.

*Shang or Western Chou Dynasty, *Pendant in the Shape of an Animal Head,* lapis lazuli, 1965.465.

*T'ang Dynasty, *Seated Figure of the Bodhisattva Mañjuśrī,* gilt bronze, 1965.467.

T'ang Dynasty, *Mask,* bronze, 1927.14.

T'ang Dynasty, *Mirror,* bronze, 1955.140.

Indo-Chinese Sculpture and Painting

Annamese(?), fourteenth century or later, *Head,* stone, 1965.468.

*Cambodian, tenth-eleventh century, *Buddhist Divinity,* stone, 1943.1.

*Cambodian, Khmer Period, *Head of a Buddha,* stone, 1928.165.

Siamese, Buddhist, eighteenth-nineteenth century, *Paradise,* 1965.464.

Japanese Painting and Sculpture

*Fujiwara Period, *Votive Plaque,* bronze, 1955.139.
Japanese, *Halo for Buddhist Figure,* polychromed wood, 1948.43.
Japanese, fourteenth century, *Yakushi and the Generals,* 1940.59.
Japanese, twentieth century, *Bird on Bamboo Branch,* 1948.84.

Medieval Art

African(?), *Crucifix,* iron, 1950.120.
*French Romanesque, twelfth century, *Scenes from the Story of Samson,* marble capital, 1922.132.
French, thirteenth century, *Head of Male Saint,* 1965.471.
French, *Blue Glass from Chartres,* 1942.232.
French, *Two Fragments of Chartres Glass,* 1925.14.1-2.
Medieval, *Vellum Leaf from a Hymnal,* 1965.485.
Medieval(?), *Bracteate Coin,* gold, 1942.230.
Spanish(?) Gothic, *Head and Shoulders of Madonna,* wood, 1965.475.

American Painting and Sculpture

Chapin, James, *Tumble-down Barn,* 1961.120.
Coletti, Joseph A., *Head of a Child,* marble, 1948.56.
Farrer, Thomas C., copy after Turner, *The Fighting Temeraire,* 1965.445.
James, William, *Winter Landscape,* 1949.15.
Levine, Jack, *King Asa,* 1953; 1965.446.
Luce, Molly, *The Centennial,* 1927; 1948.41.
Manship, Paul, *Wrestlers,* bronze, 1928.163.
Manship, Paul, *Centaur and Nymph,* bronze, 1928.164.
Moore, Charles H., *Portrait of John Ruskin,* 1965.447.
Mower, Martin, *Flower Still-life,* 1949.73.
Nakamura, Kanji, *Portrait of Dr. Denman W. Ross,* 1938.125.
Rosenberg, James N., *Slender Birch,* 1965.448.
Ross, Denman W., *Portrait of Miss Nathurst,* 1926; 1948.42.
Ruellan, Andrée, *New England Port,* 1961.125.
Sterne, Maurice, *Two Priests,* 1911; 1965.449.

Flemish and Spanish Painting

Isenbrandt, Adriaen, *St. John,* 1955.165.
*Juan de Burgos, *Annunciation,* 1928.168.
*Master of St. Gudule, *Christ in the Garden of Gethsemane,* 1950.41.

French Painting and Sculpture

Courbet, Gustave, attributed to, *Portrait of a Boy,* 1949.13.
French School, fifteenth century, *Crucifixion,* 1928.167.
*Poussin, Nicolas, *The Holy Family,* ca. 1650-51; 1942.168.
*Poussin, Nicolas, *The Infant Bacchus Entrusted to the Nymphs,* 1657; 1942.167.
Richier, Ligier(?), *Christ with Crown of Thorns,* limestone, 1927.17.2.

German Painting and Sculpture

Cranach, Lucas, *Portrait of Luther,* 1955.164.
German(?), *Head of a Bearded Man,* wood, 1949.27.

Italian Painting and Sculpture

Byzantine, *Virgin and Child,* 1927.27.
Fiorentino, Pier Francesco, *Madonna and Child,* 1965.458.
Francesco di Giorgio, *Madonna and Child,* 1958.284.
Giovanni di Paolo, *St. John,* 1957.8.
Italian, thirteenth century, *Crucifixion,* 1957.202.
Italian, fifteenth century, *Bust of a Child,* terra cotta, 1965.474.
Italian, *Bust of the Madonna and Child,* terra cotta, 1965.472.
Italian, seventeenth century, *Coat of Arms,* travertine, 1926.31.1.
Italian, *Mortar,* bronze, 1965.494.
Italian, *Mother and Child,* marble, 1965.473.
*Lorenzetti, Ambrogio, *Crucifixion,* 1939.113.
*Master of the Fogg Pietà, fourteenth century, *Mourning over the Body of Christ,* 1927.306.
*Osservanza Master, *Christ in Limbo,* 1922.172.
Paris Master, fifteenth century, *Judgment of Paris,* 1928.169.
*Tintoretto, Jacopo Robusti called, *Allegory of Fidelity,* ca. 1578; 1942.165.

American Drawings

Abbey, Edwin A., *Austen Dobson Winding up Edwin Abbey to Draw a Bookplate for Him,* 1948.93.
Aldrich, William T., *Study of a Girl,* 1965.100.
Aldrich, William T., *Two Sketches: Sailboat, Man in Uniform,* 1965.101.
Aldrich, William T., *Constance,* 1965.102.
Austin, Arthur Everett, Jr., *Seated Youth,* 1930; 1965.103.
*Bellows, George W., *Study for Portrait of his Daughter, Lady Jean,* 1965.104.
Bellows, George W., *Portrait Sketch of Mrs. Tyler,* 1919; 1965.105.
Berman, Eugene, *Les Trois Ponts* (Venice), 1965.106.
Berman, Eugene, *Landscape with Cart,* 1937; 1965.443.
Beveridge, Eliot P., *Waterfront,* 1941; 1943.34.
Cadmus, Paul, *Inventor,* 1965.107.
Calder, Alexander, *Hippopotamus,* 1965.444.
Cesare, O. E., *Reprisal,* 1924.138.

Levine, Jack, *Portrait of Ruth Gikow* (Mrs. Levine), 1965.127.
Lewandowski, Edmund D., *The Bridge*, 1952; 1961.121.
Luce, Molly, *Still Life*, 1936; 1949.14.
Marin, John, *Trinity Church*, New York, 1948.39.
Miles, Emily Winthrop, *Stylized Plant Form*, 1965.128.
Newman, Henry R., *Seascape*, 1961.124.
Pach, Walter, *Nude Female*, 1928; 1965.129.
Pach, Walter, *Portrait of Maria Modesta Martinez* (an Otomi Girl), 1965.130.
Pickhardt, Carl, *Head of Man with Hat*, 1948.68.
Pickhardt, Carl, *Standing Man*, 1948.69.
Pickhardt, Carl, *Standing Man with Mustache*, 1948.70.
Pickhardt, Carl, *Artist's Sister Agatha*, 1948.71.
Pickhardt, Carl, *Woman Wearing Hat*, 1948.72.
Pickhardt, Carl, *Five Clowns*, 1948.73.
Pickhardt, Carl, *Three Figures*, 1948.74.
Pickhardt, Carl, *Subway*, 1948.75.
Pickhardt, Carl, *Artist's Younger Sister*, 1948.76.
Pickhardt, Carl, *Artist's Brother, Fowler*, 1948.77.
Pickhardt, Carl, *Study of Two Bathers*, 1951.111.
Pickhardt, Carl, *Seated Man* (Portrait of Jack Levine), 1965.131.
Pickhardt, Carl, *Imaginary Head*, 1965.132.
Pickhardt, Carl, *Female Nude*, 1965.133.
Pickhardt, Carl, *Head of a Woman*, 1965.134.
Pickhardt, Carl, *Caricature*, 1965.135.
Polonsky, Arthur, *Head of a Young Girl*, 1965.136.
Polonsky, Arthur, *Head of a Woman*, 1965.137.
Pope, Arthur, *Portrait of Denman W. Ross*, 1950.119.
Pope, Arthur, *View of New York*, 1920; 1965.138.
Ross, Denman W., *Head of a Girl*, 1965.139.
Rowland, Benjamin, Jr., *Maine, House on Hill*, 1941; 1948.65.
Rowland, Benjamin, Jr., *The Quick and the Dead*, 1948; 1949.72.
Rubinstein, Lewis W., *Nude*, 1961.126.
Rubinstein, Lewis W., *View of Policeman from Rear*, 1965.140.
Ruellan, Andrée, *Buildings*, 1965.141.
Russell, Gordon, *Rovello*, 1957.69.
Russell, Gordon, *Hercules*, 1965.142.
Russell, Gordon, *Satyr*, 1965.143.
Russell, Gordon, *Standing Woman Draped*, 1965.144.
Sargent, Margaret, *Head of a Woman*, 1965.145.
Sargent, Margaret, *Portrait of a Man*, 1965.146.
Seligman, Kurt, *Caterpillar*, 1952; 1965.147.
Shahn, Ben, *Blind Botanist*, 1955.160.
Shahn, Ben, *Alphabet*, 1955.161.
*Shahn, Ben, *Man Picking Wheat*, 1955.162.
Shahn, Ben, *Sacco and Vanzetti*, 1956.184.
Shahn, Jonathan, *Man Seated at Table*, 1956.189.
Shahn, Jonathan, *Standing Man*, 1956.190.
Shahn, Jonathan, *Two Men at Table*, 1956.191.

*Sheeler, Charles, *Totems in Steel*, 1935; 1965.148.
Sloan, John, *McSorley's Cats*, 1965.149.
Solovioff, Nicolas, *Portrait of Hedda Gazzotti*, 1965.150.
Soyer, Raphael, *Figure Studies*, 1965.151.
Speicher, Eugene, *Head of a Girl*, 1965.152.
Speicher, Eugene, *Portrait of a Girl*, 1965.153.
Speicher, Eugene, *Study of John Hommell*, 1965.154.
Steinberg, Saul, *The Violinist*, 1965.155.
Sterne, Maurice, *Balinese Dancer*, 1965.156.
Stuempfig, Walter, *Sea Isle City*, 1965.157.
Stuempfig, Walter, *Homage to Eakins*, 1965.450.
Swetzoff, Seymour, *The Initiate*, 1949.48.
Tanguy, Yves, *Abstraction*, 1949; 1965.442.
Weber, Max, *Venice—Osteria con Cucina*, 1965.158.
Weber, Max, *Italian Landscape*, 1965.159.
Weber, Max, *Interior of a Church* (San Marco?), 1965.160.
Weber, Max, *Seated Figure*, 1917; 1965.161.
Webster, Herman A., *Campidoglio*, 1948.64.
Webster, Herman A., *Portrait of Carlotta de Felice*, 1965.162.
Webster, Herman A., *Street in Bourges or Rouen*, 1965.163.
Webster, Herman A., *Grand Central Excavations*, 1965.164 and 1965.166.
Webster, Herman A., *Street and Clock Tower at Rouen*, 1965.165.
Webster, Herman A., *Salamanca*, 1932; 1965.167.

British Drawings

Allom, Thomas, *Dinant on the Meuse*, 1965.170.
Blake, William, *The Stoning of Achan*, 1959.162.
Bone, Muirhead, *Study for the Etching "Spanish Good Friday,"* 1965.171.
Bone, Muirhead, *Street Scene*, 1965.172.
Bone, Muirhead, *Hyde Park at Marble Arch*, 1965.173.
Chinnery, George, *Sampan*, 1965.174.
Constable, John, *Three Pages from a Sketchbook*, 1965.176.
Constable, John, attributed to, *Salisbury Cathedral*, 1965.175.
Cruikshank, George, *A Penny, Sir!*, 1949.41.
Gainsborough, Thomas, *Landscape with Mounted Figures*, 1965.177.
Hoppner, John, *Man Seated*, facing left (Henry Fuseli), 1965.178.
John, Augustus, *Study of a Fishergirl at Equihen*, 1965.179.
Keene, Charles, *Two Illustrations for "Punch,"* 1965.180 and 1965.181.
Keene, Charles, *Study of Grouse*, 1965.182.
Keene, Charles, *Scene at the Beach*, 1965.183.
Landseer, Sir Edwin H., *Study of a Tiger;* verso: *Study of a Lion*, 1965.451.
Lear, Edward, *Monte Rotondo*, 1965.184.
Lely, Sir Peter, *Study of a Draped Figure*, 1965.185.
*Lely, Sir Peter, *Two Poor Knights of Windsor*, 1965.186.
*Moore, Henry, *Study for the Northampton Madonna*, 1958.24.
Moore, Henry, *Three Standing Figures;* verso: *Seated Female Figure*, 1948; 1965.187.

Nicholson, Ben, *Landscape from San Gimignano*, 1950; 1965.189.
Piper, John, *Three Landscapes, Views of Traeta Mawr*, 1965.190.
Piper, John, *Copy of Giorgione's "Tempesta,"* 1952; 1965.452.
Richardson, Jonathan, *Self Portrait*, 1965.191.
Richardson, Jonathan, *Portrait of the Artist's Son*, 1965.192.
Rossetti, Dante Gabriel, *Portrait of Mrs. Lushington*, 1965.193.
Ruskin, John, *Castle, Lucerne*, 1949.30a.
Ruskin, John, *Street Scene*, 1949.30b.
Stothard, Thomas, *Group of Figures*, 1948.94.
Sutherland, Graham, *Study for Standing Forms*, 1950; 1965.194.
Swan, John M., *Two Leopards*, 1965.195.
Turner, J. M. W., *Fish*, 1923.34.
Turner, J. M. W., *Study of a Gurnet*, 1965.453.
Turner, J. M. W., *View in Cumberland*, 1923.33.
Ward, James, *Boats and Fish*, 1965.196.
Wilkie, Sir David, *Group of Ladies*, 1965.197.
Wint, Peter de, *Landscape*, 1965.198.

Dutch Drawings

Berchem, Claes, attributed to, *The Ferry*, 1965.199.
Bisschop, Jan de, *The Wagon*, 1965.200.
Bloemaert, Abraham, *Autumn*, 1965.201.
Cort, Cornelis, *An Italian Landscape*, 1965.202.
Everdingen, Allart van, *Peasants Reaping Grain*, 1965.203.
*Gheyn, Jacques de, II, *Cross-bowman Assisted by a Milkmaid*, 1953.86.
*Goyen, Jan van, *On the Seashore*, 1965.204.
Heemskerk, Martin van, *Three Heroes of the Old Testament*, 1965.205.
Hulswit, Jan, *Landscape with Seated Figure and Horse*, 1954.98.
Leyden, Lucas van(?), *Man Riding a Steer*, 1965.206.
Maes, Nicolaas, *Head of an Old Woman*, 1965.207.
Molyn, Pieter, the Elder, *The Fowlers*, 1965.208.
Muyden, E. van, *Lion Attacking a Buffalo*, 1965.209.
Ostade, Adrian van, *Interior of an Inn*, 1965.210.
Ostade, Isaak van, *A Peasant's Cottage*, 1965.211.
Ovens, Juriaen, *Adoration of the Magi*, 1965.212.
*Rembrandt van Rijn, *Three Studies of a Child and One of an Old Woman*, 1949.4.
*Rembrandt van Rijn, *A Woman Ill in Bed with a Child*, 1961.151.
Rembrandt van Rijn, *Standing Old Man* (Blind Tobit?), 1965.213.
Van der Ulft, Jacob, *A Fortified Seaport*, 1689; 1965.214.
*Velde, Willem van de, *Two Men-of-War at Anchor with Three Small Boats*, 1965.215.
*Velde, Willem van de, *Seascape with Three Men-of-War, a Galliot, and Several Small Boats*, 1965.216.
Visscher, Cornelis, *Bust of a Boy*, 1965.217.
Visscher, Cornelis, *The Gypsy*, 1965.218.
Waterloo, Anthonie, *A Forest at Twilight*, 1965.219.

Eastern European Drawings

Archipenko, Alexander, *Female Nude*, 1965.438.
Halmi, Arthur L., *Hungarian Peasant Woman*, 1886; 1949.47.
Jacovleff, Alexandras, *Head of a Chinese Man*, 1919; 1965.439.
Michalowski, Piotr, *Artilleryman Leading his Horse into the Field*, 1965.286.
Simkohvitch, Simka, *Head Mounted on a Pedestal*, 1965.461.
Simkohvitch, Simka, *Standing Figure of a Woman*, 1965.462.
Simkohvitch, Simka, *Figure of a Dwarf Standing Beside a Table*, 1965.463.
Tchelichew, Pavel, *Frederick Ashton*, 1959.165.
*Tchelichew, Pavel, *Nicolas Kopeikine*, 1959.166.

Flemish Drawings

Brueghel, Pieter, Follower of, *A Cripple in a Cart Drawn by a Peasant*, 1965.220.
*Dyck, Anton van, *Don Carlos Coloma*, 1961.150.
*Dyck, Anton van, *A Suit of Armor*, 1954.126.
Dyck, Anton van, attributed to, *Head of a Horse*, 1965.221.
Dyck, Anton van, Follower of, *Seated Old Man*, 1952.74.
Flemish, fifteenth century, *Head of a Monk*, 1965.222.
Flemish, sixteenth century, *Study for a St. Sebastian(?)*, 1965.223.
Flemish, seventeenth century, *The Mocking of Christ*, 1965.224.
Flemish (Monogram: LDH), seventeenth century, *Portrait of a Man with a Ruff*, 1965.225.
Jordaens, Jakob, *Christ Carrying the Cross*, 1965.226.
Jordaens, Jakob, *Figure of a Standing Man*, 1965.227.
Neyts, Gillis, *Harbor Scene*, 1965.228.
*Rubens, Peter Paul, *Study for the Figure of Christ*, 1949.3.
Rubens, Peter Paul, attributed to, *Head of a Girl*, 1958.287.
Rubens, Peter Paul(?), *Study for or from "St. Ignatius Healing Those Possessed,"* 1965.229.
Uden, Lucas van, *Landscape*, 1965.230.

French Drawings

Adam, attributed to one of the family of eighteenth-century decorators, *Study for a Statue of a Seated Minerva*, 1951.117.
Andreu, Mariano, *Three Bathing Women*, 1965.232.
Blanchard, Jacques, *Charity*, 1965.233.
Boilly, Louis L.(?), *Family Portrait with Six Busts*, 1965.234.·
*Boucher, François, *Reclining Nude*, 1965.235.
Boyvin, René, *Death of Adonis*, 1965.236.
Champaigne, Philippe de, attributed to, *Head of a Nun*, 1965.238.
Chapuy, Nicolas, *La Tour St. Jacques et la Boucherie*, Paris, 1965.239.
Charlet, Nicolas-Toussaint, *Guignol*, 1965.454.
Chasseriau, Théodore, *Portrait of Madame Mottez*, 1965.240.
Claude Gellée, called le Lorrain, *A Wooded Hillside*, 1965.241.

Claude Gellée, called le Lorrain, *Achilles' Mother Entrusting Achilles to the Centaur Chiron*, 1965.242.

Claude, Follower of, *Roman Landscape*, 1965.231.

*Clodion, *Reclining Bacchante Holding a Vase*, 1965.243.

*Clouet, François, *Portrait of Claude Gouffier de Boisy*, 1949.5.

Colson, Jean-François Gilles, called, *A Young Girl Asleep*, 1965.244.

*Corot, Jean-Baptiste-Camille, *Henry Leroy as a Child*, 1965.245.

*Corot, Jean-Baptiste-Camille, *View of Mount Soracte from Cività Castellana*, 1965.247.

Corot, Jean-Baptiste-Camille, *Woman Knitting*, 1965.246.

Courbet, Gustave, *Portrait of Trapadoux*(?), 1965.248.

Coypel, Antoine, *Nude Figure of a Man;* verso: *Studies of Drapery*, 1965.249.

*Daumier, Honoré, *Two Lawyers Conversing*, 1965.250.

Degas, Edgar, *René de Gas, Convalescent*, 1965.251.

Degas, Edgar, *Copy After van Dyck's "Margaret of Lorraine,"* 1955.2.

Degas, Edgar, *A Young Woman Reclining in a Chair, an Open Book on Her Lap*, 1965.252.

*Degas, Edgar, *Study for the Portrait of Madame Hertel* (La Dame aux Chrysanthèmes), 1865; 1965.253.

*Degas, Edgar, *Study for the Portrait of Madame Julie Burtin*, 1863; 1965.254.

*Degas, Edgar, *Study for Portrait of Diego Martelli*, 1879; 1965.255.

Degas, Edgar, *Study for Portarit of Diego Martelli* (full length), 1965.256.

Degas, Edgar, *After the Bath*, 1965.257.

Degas, Edgar, *After the Bath*, 1965.258.

*Degas, Edgar, *After the Bath*, 1965.259.

*Degas, Edgar, *Young Woman in Street Costume of the Time*, 1965.260.

*Degas, Edgar, *Portrait Sketch of Edouard Manet*, 1965.261.

Degas, Edgar, *A Nude Figure Bathing*, 1965.262.

*Degas, Edgar, *A Ballet Dancer in Position Facing Three-quarters Front*, 1872; 1965.263.

Degas, Edgar, *Sketches of Dancers*, 1965.264.

Degas, Edgar, *Madonna and Child*, 1965.265.

Degas, Edgar, *Portrait of a Young Girl* (Giovanna Bellelli?), 1965.266.

Degas, Edgar(?), *Self Portrait*, 1955.163.

Delacroix, Eugène, *Francis I and His Mistress*, 1965.267.

*Delacroix, Eugène, *Mounted Arab Attacking a Panther*, 1965.268.

Delacroix, Eugène, *Arab on Horseback Attacked by Lion*, 1965.269.

Delacroix, Eugène, *Hamlet and His Mother*, 1965.270.

Delacroix, Eugène, *Anne of Cleves* (after Holbein), 1965.271.

Delacroix, Eugène, *Camel*, 1965.272.

*Delacroix, Eugène, *Portrait of Frederic Villot*, 1949.6.

Delamain, Paul, *Man on Horseback Firing a Gun*, 1965.273.

Deshayes, Célestin, *Fashion Plate: Three Ladies in Period Dresses*, 1965.455.

Fantin-Latour, Henri, *Self Portrait*, 1871; 1965.274.

Fontainebleau, School of, *Mythological Scene*, 1965.275.

*Fragonard, Jean-Honoré, *Woman Standing with Hand on Hip*, 1965.276.

French, seventeenth century, *Head of a Man*, 1965.278.

French, seventeenth(?) century, *Scene in an American Indian Teepee*, 1965.237.

French, eighteenth century, *An Ecclesiastic*, 1965.279.

French, eighteenth century, *Studies of an Ecclesiastic*, 1777; 1965.280.

French, nineteenth century, *The Ravages of War*, 1965.281.

French, nineteenth century, *Woman Holding a Mirror*, 1965.282.

Fresnaye, Roger de la, *Chef de Musique*, 1959.141.

*Gauguin, Paul, *Head of a Peasant Girl*, 1965.283.

Gavarni, *The Latest News*, 1965.284.

*Géricault, Théodore, *Negro Soldier Holding a Lance*, 1965.285.

*Géricault, Théodore, *An Italian Landscape*, 1965.287.

Giraud, Eugène, *Two Figures* (Arabs), 1965.288.

Gogh, Vincent van, *The Wounded Veteran*, 1882; 1965.289.

Greuze, Jean-Baptiste, *Seated Nude Woman*, 1965.290.

*Greuze, Jean-Baptiste, *A Kneeling Youth with Outstretched Arms*, 1965.291.

Grévin, Alfred, *Standing Female Nude and Attendant*, 1965.292.

Grévin, Alfred, *Artist at his Easel and Two Ladies Conversing*, 1965.293.

Guys, Constantin, *The Amazon*, 1959.163.

Ibels, Henri Gabriel, *Circus*, design for a fan, 1965.456.

*Ingres, J. A. D., *Portrait of Madame Hayard, née Jeanne Suzanne Allion*, 1965.298.

Ingres, J. A. D., *Four Figure Studies After Andrea del Sarto*, 1965.297.

Ingres, J. A. D., *Virgil Reading the Aeneid to Augustus*, 1965.299.

*Ingres, J. A. D., *A Crouching Nude Youth Reaching for a Stone, Separate Study of Arm*, 1965.296.

*Ingres, J. A. D., *Portrait of Madame d'Haussonville*, 1965.294.

*Ingres, J. A. D., *Study for the Portrait of Madame d'Haussonville*, 1965.295.

Isabey, Eugène, *Sailboat*, 1953.5.

Isabey, Eugène, *Shipwreck*, 1953.6.

Isabey, Eugène, *Harbor Scene*, 1953.7.

Jacque, Charles, *Children Feeding Chickens*, 1965.300.

Jouvenet, Jean-Baptiste, *A Saintly Cleric Healing the Sick*, 1965.301.

Lagneau, Nicolas, *Portrait of a Man*, 1965.302.

Lorraine, School of, *St. Catherine of Alexandria*, 1965.277.

Lydis, Mariette, *La Dormeuse*, 1928; 1965.303.

Lydis, Mariette, *The Annunciation*, 1927; 1965.457.

*Manet, Édouard, *Interior of a Café*, 1965.304.

Masson, André, *Man with Mandolin*, 1965.305.

Matisse, Henri, *Two Girl Musicians*, 1965.306.

*Matisse, Henri, *A Lady with a Necklace*, 1965.307.

Meissonier, Ernest, *A Suit of Armor*, 1965.308.

Meissonier, Ernest, *A Suit of Armor*, 1965.309.

Millet, Jean-François, *Offering to Pan*, 1965.310.

*Millet, Jean-François, *Marguerite Sensier, as a Baby*, 1965.311.

*Millet, *Portrait of Mme. Alfred Sensier*, 1963.144.

Monet, Claude, *Two Men Fishing*, 1965.312.

Natoire, Charles, *Mercury Confiding the Infant Bacchus to the Nymphs*, 1955.133.

Oudry, Jean-Baptiste, *Head of a Monkey*, 1955.13.

Pajou, Augustin, *Mother and Child at an Open Window*, 1965.313.

Parrocel, Pierre, *Figure Studies of a Child*, 1965.314.

Patel, Pierre Antoine(?), *Ox-cart in a Wind-swept Landscape*, 1965.315.

Pissarro, Camille, *Peasant Girl Sitting*, ca. 1885; 1965.323.
Pissarro, Camille, *Le Marché à Pontoise*, 1965.324.
Poussin, School of, *Bacchanal*, 1965.325.
*Prud'hon, Pierre-Paul, *A Nymph Teased by Cupids;* verso: *Nude Man*, 1965.326.
Raffet, Auguste, *Study for "La Caricature,"* 1831; 1965.327.
Redon, Odilon, *The Raising of Lazarus*, 1955.132.
*Redon, Odilon, *Don Quixote*, 1965.328.
Rodin, Auguste, *Seated Nude*, 1918.43.
Rodin, Auguste, *Seated Nude*, 1918.44.
Rodin, Auguste, *A Dancing Cambodian Figure*, 1965.329.
Rops, Félicien, *Bust of a Woman*, 1965.330.
Rousseau, Théodore, *Landscape*, 1965.331.
Rousseau, Théodore, *Forest at Fontainebleau*, 1965.332.
Segonzac, André Dunoyer de, *Head of a Woman*, 1965.333.
Thomas, Jean-Baptiste (?), *The Dying Paris Rejected by Oenone*, 1965.334.
Troyon, Constant, *Goats*, 1955.1.
Valadon, Suzanne, *A Nude Girl Reclining on a Couch*, 1965.335.
Villon, Jacques, *Three Kings*, 1955.150.
*Watteau, Antoine, *Six Studies of Heads*, 1965.336.

German and Austrian Drawings

Aachen, Hans von, copy after, *Diana and Actaeon*, 1965.337.
Beckmann, Max, *Head of Woman*, 1956.27.
Beckmann, Max, *Portrait of Mrs. Swarzenski*, 1956.28.
Corinth, Lovis, *Self Portrait*, 1956.29.
*Cranach, Lucas, *St. Anthony Abbot*, 1965.338.
*Dürer, Albrecht, *Susanna of Bavaria*, 1949.1.
*Dürer, Albrecht, *Lamentation*, 1521; 1965.339.
Elsheimer, Adam, *Study of Three Warriors*, 1956.342.
*German, fourteenth century, *Two Designs for Illuminated Initials*, 1954.127.
German, sixteenth century, *The Birth of the Virgin*, copied from Dürer's woodcut, 1965.340.
German, sixteenth century, *Apocalypse*, copy after Dürer's woodcut of the Four Winds, 1965.341.
Glockendon, Albrecht, *Ecce Homo*, 1965.343.
*Hollar, Wenceslaus, *Shore with Boats*, 1965.344.
Hofer, Karl, *Dancers*, 1956.36.
*Holbein, Hans, the Younger, *Portrait of a Leper* (so-called), 1949.2.
Kulmbach, Hans von, *St. Nicholas*, 1965.345.
Menzel, Adolph, *Head of a Man*, 1965.346.
*Menzel, Adolph, *Portrait of an Elderly Man in a Military Topcoat*, 1965.347.
Monogrammist C B, *The Annunciation*, 1965.348.
Müntz, Johann Heinrich, *Landscape with Figures*, 1965.188.
Nolde, Emil, *Head of Man*, 1956.30.
Pencz, Georg, *The Prodigal Son*, 1965.349.
Richter, Ludwig, *Home-coming*, 1965.350.
*Schäufelein, Hans Leonhard, *Adoration of the Magi*, 1965.351.

Springer, Ferdinand, *Studies of Male Nudes*, 1965.168.
Springer, Ferdinand, *A Standing Woman Holding a Child*, 1965.169.
Stimmer, Tobias, copy after, *Crucifixion*, 1965.352.
Strigel, Bernhard, *St. Agatha*, 1959.158.

Italian Drawings

Abbate, Niccolò dell', Follower of, *A Concert*, 1965.353.
Balestra, Antonio, *Adoration of the Magi*, 1955.14.
Baroccio(?), Federigo, *Rest on the Flight into Egypt*, 1965.354.
Baroccio, School of, *The Annunciation*, 1965.355.
*Fra Bartolommeo, *Madonna and Child with a Kneeling Angel*, 1965.356.
Fra Bartolommeo, School of, *A Flying Angel;* verso: *A Flying Angel Playing a Lute*, 1965.357.
Beccafumi, Domenico, *Study for Part of the Mosaic Frieze of the Siena Cathedral Pavement*, 1965.358.
Beccafumi, Domenico, *Head of an Old Man Turned Three-quarters Right*, 1965.359.
Bernini, Gian Lorenzo, copy after, *Truth*, 1965.360.
Bibiena, Ferdinando G., *A Roman Palace*, 1965.361.
Bison, Giuseppe Bernardino, *Choir of Angels (Music Making Angels)*, 1955.137.
Bison, Giuseppe Bernardino, *Hero Crowned with Laurel Riding a Horse*, 1965.362.
Bologna, School of, seventeenth century, *St. Francis and Brother Leo(?) Kneeling in Adoration*, 1965.363.
Bologna, School of, seventeenth century, *St. Gregory and St. Augustine*, 1965.364.
Brizzi, Francesco, *The Madonna and Child Supported in Clouds and Adored by St. Petronius and St. Francis*, 1965.365.
Cambiaso, Luca, *Diana and Callisto*, 1965.366.
Cambiaso, Luca, *St. Matthew and the Angel*, 1965.367.
Cambiaso, Luca, *Nymph and Putti Riding on a Dolphin*, 1965.368.
Cambiaso, Luca, *Christ Raising the Daughter of Jairus*, 1965.369.
Canova, Antonio, *Lady Reclining in a Chair in a Classical Pose*, 1948.25.
Caravaggio, Polidoro da, *The Bearing of the Body of Christ*, 1965.370.
Carracci, School of, *Christ's Entry into Limbo*, Copy after Dürer's woodcut, 1965.371.
Carracci, Annibale, attributed to, *Head of a Youth*, 1965.372.
Castiglione, Giovanni Benedetto, *The Nativity*, 1965.373.
Cortona, Pietro da, *Flying Figure*, 1958.286.
Cremonini, Leonardo, *Maternity*, 1951; 1965.374.
Ferrari(?), Gaudenzio, *Christ and the Apostles*, 1965.375.
Florentine, fifteenth century, *A Princess Captured by Roman Soldiers Outside the Walls of a Town*, 1965.376.
Florentine, fifteenth century, *The Princess Stabbed to Death in the Presence of a King and His Councillors*, 1965.377.
Florentine, sixteenth century, *Reclining Nude Youth;* verso: *Various Sketches*, 1965.378.
Ghezzi, Pier Luigi, *Pulcinelli*, 1948.62.
Ghezzi, Pier Luigi, *Pulcinelli*, 1948.63.

Reni, Guido, *Profile Head of a Bearded Man*, 1958.42.
Reni, Guido, Attributed to, *Head of Christ Crowned with Thorns*, 1965.412.
Ricci, Marco, *Three Men Resting Near a Pyramid*, 1965.413.
Roman School, seventeenth century, *Bacchanalian Procession*, 1965.414.
Severini, Gino, *Two Punchinellos*, 1959.164.
Severini, Gino, *Still Life*, ca. 1931; 1965.460.
Testa(?), Pietro, *Group of Figures*, 1947.26.
Tiepolo, Giovanni Battista, *Two Fauns*, 1963.143.
Tiepolo, Giovanni Battista, *Annunciation*, 1965.415.
Tiepolo, Giovanni Battista, *Design for a Ceiling Fresco*, 1965.416.
*Tiepolo, Giovanni Battista, *Holy Family Enthroned with St. Sebastian, St. Catherine of Alexandria and St. Francis*, 1965.417.
*Tiepolo, Giovanni Battista, *Rest on the Flight into Egypt*, 1965.418.
Tiepolo, Giovanni Battista, *Youth Standing Between Two Bearded Old Men*, 1965.419.
*Tiepolo, Giovanni Domenico, *The Boar Hunt*, 1965.420.
*Tiepolo, Giovanni Domenico, *Group of Punchinellos with Dancing Dogs*, 1965.421.
Tiepolo, Giovanni Domenico, *St. Ambrose*, 1965.422.
Tintoretto, Jacopo Robusti called, *Studies for a Martyrdom of St. Sebastian;* verso: *Studies of Archers*, 1965.423.
Tintoretto, Jacopo Robusti called, *Samson and the Philistine*, 1965.424.
Umbro-Florentine School, *St. Jerome*, 1959.159.
Vaccaro(?), Domenico, *Madonna of Mercy*, 1965.425.
Vaga, Perino del, *Design for an Overdoor*, 1965.426.
Vaga, Perino del, School of, *A Putto and Seated Nude Youth Playing with Lions*, 1965.427.
Venetian School, *St. John the Baptist and a Bishop-saint, Both Standing in Niches;* verso: *Death of Ananias(?)*, 1965.428.
*Venetian School, seventeenth century, *A Triumphant General Crowned by Flying Figure*, 1965.429.
*Veronese, Paolo Caliari called, *Rest on the Flight into Egypt*, 1965.430.
Vespignani, Renzo, *Girl in Bed* (Grazella), 1953; 1965.431.
Vespignani, Renzo, *Baby*, 1949; 1965.432.
Zuccaro, Federico, *Nobles Worshipping Before a Crucifix*, 1965.433.
Zuccaro, Taddeo, *Design for Overdoor Decoration*, 1965.434.

Mexican Drawings

Orozco, José Clemente, *Figure with Hands Clasped Before Face*, 1965.435.
Rivera, Diego, *Figures of Man and Woman*, 1949.23.
Rivera, Diego, *Study of a Sleeping Woman*, 1921; 1965.436.
*Rivera, Diego, *Madame Fisher*, 1965.437.
Zalce, Alfredo, *Rice Paddies*, 1961.122.

Spanish Drawings

*Goya, Francisco, *You Make a Mistake if You Marry Again*, 1949.7.
Goya, Imitator of, *Portrait of a Man*, 1965.440.

Picasso, Pablo, *A Reclining Nude*, 1965.316.
Picasso, Pablo, *A Clown*, 1965.317.
*Picasso, Pablo, *A Mother Holding a Child;* verso: *Standing Nude Man*, 1965.318.
*Picasso, Pablo, *The Bathers*, 1918; 1965.319.
Picasso, Pablo, *The Philosopher*, 1965.320.
*Picasso, Pablo, *Portrait of Fonte*, 1965.321.
Picasso, Pablo, *Portrait of a Seated Man*, 1965.322.

Prints

It has proved impossible in a catalogue this size to give the title, medium and acquisition number of the two thousand and twelve prints given or bequeathed by Paul J. Sachs. However, to give some idea of his range as a print collector, we have compiled two lists, one according to national schools and the other according to the medium in which each print was executed.

Not infrequently Mr. Sachs made a gift in conjunction with one or two friends. These gifts we have not included, but we would like to call attention to the size and interest of one such gift. In 1938, Mr. Sachs and his close friend of many years, W. G. Russell Allen, an equally passionate and enlightened print collector, presented to the Fogg Museum Print Room five hundred and sixty-seven French eighteenth-century engravings.

National Schools

American	298
Austrian	3
Bohemian	1
British	56
Canadian	1
French	741
German	441
Italian	402
Netherlandish	35
Polish	1
Russian	1
Spanish	13
Swiss	12
Anonymous	7
Total	2,012

Media

Woodcuts	1,147
Chiaroscuro Woodcuts	8
Linoleum Cuts	3
Engravings	127
Etchings	324
Aquatints	10
Mezzotints	13
Lithographs	285
Wood Engravings	30
Monotypes	3
Clichés-verre	40
Serigraph	1
Miscellaneous	21
Total	2,012

Wood blocks (1915.10-11; 1916.66)